HOUSEPLANTS 101

HOW TO CHOOSE, STYLE, GROW, AND NURTURE YOUR INDOOR PLANTS

PETER SHEPPERD

CONTENTS

THE 4 BEST EASY-CARE HOUSEPLANTS FOR YOUR HOME

And the 5 most essential indoor gardening items checklist

This checklist includes:

- The 4 best and easiest to look after houseplants that you can kick off your indoor green fingered adventure.
- 5 of the highest quality indoor gardening items that will help you bring your plants to life.
- Where you can buy these items for the lowest price.

The last thing we want is for your indoor gardening project start to be delayed because you weren't prepared.

To receive your essential indoor gardening checklist, scan the QR code below:

INTRODUCTION

You may have noticed that houseplants have all of a—sudden come back into fashion. Keeping and caring for plants indoors has gone from being something that preoccupies the older generation to a full-blown leafy love affair. Millennials, especially, fork out thousands of dollars to grow their houseplant collection.

There's no doubt that social media has played a considerable role in taking houseplants back to the glory days—the 80s. Surely, you remember your parents or grandparents tenderly watering the then-famous spider plant. Everyone had one; they make so many tiny 'spiders' that with just a few strategic snips, you could gift a small baby plant to the whole neighbourhood! Now, years later, this "sharing is caring" attitude has returned to create a new generation of plant parents. The only real difference is the fact that social media platforms now make it so much easier to connect with fellow enthusiasts.

Of course, the benefit of owning a houseplant or three isn't limited to the community you'll have access to. Actually, the advantages of indoor plants should make them a necessity and not just part of the décor. Houseplants have scientifically been proven to reduce bodily and psychological stress (Lee et al., 2015). This is especially true if you interact with your indoor plants! So, the next time someone says you're crazy because you tell your houseplants about your day, don't worry, you're the healthy one.

Some other benefits of indoor plants include:

- Enhanced job satisfaction

- Increased productivity
- Reduced stress
- Improved mood
- Improved air quality
- Enhanced cognitive health

Houseplants are so remarkable that even looking at a plant reduces blood pressure (Perry, n.d.). You may be sitting there thinking, "I know all this, but I am a plant murderer." I know, I've been there. You're so excited when you bring a plant home and promise yourself that it will be different; this time, you'll succeed as a plant parent. Then, two weeks later, your houseplant ends up in the dustbin, all yellow and drooping or dried to a crisp.

I'm here to tell you that with some basic knowledge, you will be able to surround yourself with all the greenery you can manage. All you have to do is to never give up on making your urban jungle dreams come true!

Let's get you equipped with all the know-how to not only select the perfect houseplants but also to keep them alive.

SELECTING YOUR HOUSEPLANT

You'll be happy to know that you may not be the one responsible for your plant's demise. A lot of the time, people don't check the health of the plant before they buy it. It's a case of them falling in love with the foliage, color, or flower and rushing to pay. However, if you know what to look for to make sure your plant is in good health to begin with, you're setting yourself up for success.

Shape

Look for a lovely bushy plant. This will be a good indication that the plant is pushing out new growth regularly, which is a sign of good health. Avoid buying plants that are leggy or spindly. Houseplants lose leaves when they're not happy, so a gangly plant shows that something is wrong. That doesn't exactly matter when the plant is still in the shop but taking home an already unhappy plant increases the chances of it dying a slow death.

Condition

The leaves of a plant are a good gauge of general health. You want to make sure that the plant has no signs of browning or yellowing. Floppy leaves or, alternatively, crispy leaves are also signs that the plant is not doing too well and maybe heading toward death's door.

Roots

I know a lot of people are uncomfortable with checking a plant's roots in the store. Don't be. It is your right as a customer to make sure what you plan on buying meets your standards.

You want to pull the plant out of the nursery pot and look for strong and firm roots. If some of the roots are brown mush, that points to root rot, and you definitely don't want to take that plant home. Root rot happens when a plant is watered too often. You'll read more about root rot later—it is one of the most common reasons plants don't make it, believe it or not.

If the roots are visible on top of the compost or even poking out of the drainage holes at the bottom, the plant is pot-bound. This isn't as bad as root rot, but as a beginner plant parent, don't buy it. When plants are root-bound, they struggle to thrive and won't be in the best condition.

Pests and Diseases

One thing you don't want to do, specifically if you have plants at home already, is bring pests home to infect your other houseplants. I can't stress enough that prevention is better than cure. Some pests are challenging to get rid of.

Check to see if anything is moving on and under the leaves of the plant. Some bugs don't move and just sit there, sucking the life out of the plant. These nasties can be identified through a white sticky substance, bleached or speckled foliage, or silvery-white streaks on the leaves.

Bringing Your Houseplant Home

Now that you've selected the healthiest plant possible, you have to make sure to keep it healthy. I know, this is the part you've been dreading, but don't worry, I've got you.

The four main things you have to pay attention to are your plant's lighting requirements, watering needs, the temperature, as well as humidity prerequisites. Since this depends on the type of plant you bought, I'll leave it to you to research what your houseplant needs to thrive. But, let's look at those four aspects in general and the typical mistakes new plant owners make. I'll cover each section in more detail later on.

Lighting

Plants need light to live; it is their source of energy. Some plants need more light than others, but most plants will do well in bright, indirect, or filtered light. Direct sunlight is hardly ever required unless you happen to be a succulent lover. It's best to place your plants three feet away from a north-, east-, or west-facing window. Keep in mind that light changes at different times of the year, and this may necessitate moving plants around.

Interesting fact: If you can read a book comfortably without having to squint, then there is enough light for most houseplants.

If you don't have a lot of light in your house, it doesn't mean you can't be part of the houseplant club. Later on, I will discuss plants that can tolerate lower-light conditions, making it possible for you to green even the darkest of corners.

Watering

Overwatering is the foremost plant killer. I will even go as far as to bet you that any plant casualties you've had in the past were due to too much water. I don't know why we do it, but it's as if we want to show our love for our plants through watering. In essence, we're drowning our plants with love. I can't help but chuckle. Closing the tap on overwatering was by far the most challenging aspect of successfully keeping plants when I first started.

When it comes to watering your plants, I want you to take a less is more approach. You will soon see that plants do much better underwatered than overwatered.

Temperature

Most houseplants will be just fine in the same conditions you're comfortable in. Just as humans, most plants prefer it warm during the day and cooler at night. Keep in mind that plants don't enjoy major fluctuations in temperature. That is why you don't want to place your plant near a radiator or air-conditioning unit, in a drafty area, or on a windowsill.

Humidity

Another important factor often overlooked by new plant parents is the moisture in the air. Most houseplants need more humidity than what the average home can offer, especially when centrally heated. Kitchens and bathrooms are usually more humid than other areas of the home, so I suggest placing plants that require more moisture in these rooms. Alternatively, you can raise the humidity by filling a tray with pebbles, pouring water to the level of the pebbles, and placing your plant on top. The water will produce moisture as it evaporates.

If you pay particular attention to these four aspects, you will create an environment for your houseplants to thrive in, which will, in turn, lead to a pleased plant parent!

Next, I will cover, in more detail, what your houseplants need to stay alive, plants that do well indoors, easy-care vs high-maintenance plants, how to style your plants, and other informative topics that will turn that murderous thumb of yours green.

1

HOW TO CARE FOR HOUSEPLANTS

There are a lot of houseplants available that are easy to grow. We fail to keep them alive because we don't know what they need in order to thrive. Plants start out in a greenhouse—a space where the conditions are ideal for them to grow and remain healthy. However, outside of the greenhouse is another ball game altogether.

When you first bring your plant home, there will be an adjustment period. During this time, your plant may look worse for wear, but with the right care, it will bounce back quickly. The trick is to imitate the climate your plant originally comes from. For example, tropical plants need warm, humid environments, while succulents come from hot, dry climates. It will take some research on your part to find the exact requirements for each plant you bring home.

You know your home, the humidity, temperature, light conditions, etc. You will need to consider this with each plant you intend to bring home. Think about it this way; you can't expect to keep succulents indoors when you don't have a sunny enough spot to put them in. That is speeding down the road to hotel failure.

Once you select a plant you know will acclimate to your home environment easily, it is time to get yourself up to date with watering requirements. It's here where things may get a little tricky.

WATERING NEEDS

As you know by now, overwatering is the number one cause of houseplant death. New plant parents always fear that they're not watering enough without realizing that plants don't like wet feet. Roots that are saturated to such a point that it gets mushy mean one thing—it's the end.

I know that it is difficult at first to tell when your plants need water. One way I did it before I got to know each plant's individual needs is by testing its weight. If you pick up the container and it is very light, it means your plant needs a drink. If it is on the heavy side, the soil is moist enough to meet your plant's watering needs, and you should not add more water.

Most houseplants prefer being on the dry side. In the same breath, I need to add that letting your plant get to the point where they wilt due to dehydration is also not a good thing. This causes undue stress on your plant and can also damage the roots. If this does happen, move your plant to a shady area and place it in a bowl filled with lukewarm water. Soak it for 30 minutes and let drain. You may have to weigh the pot down with some rocks if it floats.

Signs of Overwatering

- Fungus or mold on the soil
- Mushy and even stinky roots
- Dropping of young and old leaves
- Brown, rotten patches on leaves

Signs of Underwatering

- Slow growth
- Translucent leaves
- Dropping of leaves and flowers
- Brown, yellow, or curled leaf edges

HOW TO WATER YOUR PLANTS

Some plants, such as African violet, Cyclamens, and Peperomia, hate water on their leaves. Luckily, there are different methods of watering your plants to fit their temperaments. You may think I am anthropomorphizing plants by attributing them tempers, but just you wait and see how dramatic some houseplants can be if their needs aren't met!

Before we look at the various methods you can use to water your plants, remember to always water with lukewarm water to avoid temperature shock. Hard tap water should be avoided as the chemicals may harm your plants. You can leave a bucket outside to collect rainwater, or if that isn't possible, let tap water stand for 24 hours before watering.

From Above

Most plants will do just fine with watering from above. You want to give enough water so that it drains out of the bottom. See that as a sign to stop watering. This is one sure-fire way to know that the soil is evenly moist, and your plant's roots will have access to a drink. Let the excess water drain away.

From Below

This is the preferred method if you don't want to splash water on a plant's leaves. Place the plant in a saucer filled with water for 30 minutes. Afterwards, lift the pot and let the excess water drain before placing your plant back in its usual spot.

Dip and Drain

Similar to watering from below, drip and drain is an excellent technique for watering orchids. Instead of using a saucer, use a container the same depth as the plant's nursery pot. Fill the container with tepid water, but make sure it will not overflow the top of the nursery pot. All you then have to do is place your houseplant in the container and wait 10 minutes. When done, let it drain thoroughly.

You may have noted that drainage is often mentioned. It is a vital facet of healthy houseplants. Always choose a container with drainage holes and use potting soil correctly mixed to offer indoor plants excellent drainage. More on that later.

I don't suggest sticking to a watering timetable. The main problem with this method is that it doesn't allow for the different needs of your plants. Yes, a watering schedule of once or twice a week may be perfectly fine for most plants, but not always. It is best to get to know your plants' needs instead. If the top half to three-quarters of an inch of soil is dry, most plants will be happy to get offered a drink at this time. The same can't be said of water-wise plants like Sansevieria, Aloe, or Succulents, which like to dry out completely before the next watering.

WHAT TO FEED YOUR INDOOR PLANTS

Plants need more than just water—they need food to thrive. After bringing your plant home, wait a week or two before feeding it. You should always give your plants time to adjust to the new environment before adding extra stress like repotting or feeding.

When the plant has acclimatized, you can add a liquid houseplant feed the next time you water your plant and from then on, once a month. In colder months, you'll want to stop feeding your plants since they won't actively be growing during this time.

When feeding your plant, always follow the manufacturer's instructions. You may be tempted to give a little extra, but over-feeding can damage the plant. It's also best to feed when the soil is already moist. The reason is two-fold. Firstly, you don't want a thirsty plant to suck up fertilizer when it's actually craving water. It will most likely give your plant a shock. Secondly, if the soil is already moist, the plant food will reach the roots directly and won't immediately drain away.

If you're afraid you'll end up overfeeding your plant or completely forget to, you can consider using slow-release pellets or spikes. This is a more low-maintenance approach where a little bit of food will be released every time you water.

Some extra care ideas you can add to your weekly watering session include wiping your plant's leaves, removing old leaves and dead flowers, and inspecting the plant for pests or disease.

MAKING SURE YOUR HOUSEPLANTS GET THE BEST LIGHT

Plants need light like we need food. It is their source of energy and helps with carrying out biological processes like photosynthesis. The amount of light each plant needs depends on the type of plant, but I am sure you thought as much. To understand how much light a plant will need, look at their native habitat. Do you find them out in the open, savoring the sun, or underneath a canopy of green where they only receive heavily filtered light? Based on this, you'll be able to figure out where in your home they will be happy.

Most of the time, when you buy a plant, it will have a label mentioning watering needs as well as the best light conditions for optimal growth. Let's look at the different natural light settings.

Full Sun

You won't easily find a houseplant that likes full sun. Directly sunlight for prolonged periods will damage most plants. Leaf burn is a reality. Also, with such heat, most plants will dry out quickly. If you don't check regularly, you'll find yourself staring at a dried-up version of your cherished houseplant sooner rather than later. Desert cacti are exceptions; they enjoy the heat of the sun.

Partial Sunlight

You may have wondered why I didn't mention succulents under full sun. Well, although they can tolerate full sun, they actually prefer some sun and bright, indirect light. If you place a plant close to a west- or east-facing window, it will receive some morning or evening sun without experiencing the extreme heat of the midday sun. Flowering plants thrive in these lighting conditions.

Full Shade or Low Light

Plants that like these conditions are perfect beginner plants, specifically because plants that like low light usually require infrequent watering. That is just what you need if you're a recovering over waterer (yeah, that's a thing). Some plants that do well in low-light conditions include ZZ plant, Sansevieria, Dragon Tree, and Cast Iron plant.

Bright, Indirect Light

Most houseplants will fall under this category. Large east- and west-facing windows are perfect for plants that need bright light to thrive. Just remember not to place your plants too close to any window.

If a plant doesn't get the right amount of light, it won't necessarily die; it just won't grow. But there are other ways your plants will show you they are not getting enough or are getting too much light.

Signs of not enough light

- Flowers won't bloom
- Weak growth
- Plant looks lanky
- Yellow leaves which will eventually drop
- New leaves remain small

Signs of too much light

- Flowers die quickly
- Leaves dry out
- Color of leaves are faded
- Leaves look wilted

Then again, is anything ever as simple as just looking at a list and knowing exactly what is wrong? All the signs mentioned that indicate either too little or too much light can also be caused by a handful of other things. This is why it is so important to get to know your plants; you will then, through a process of elimination, be able to tell what is causing any deterioration.

You may also notice that your plant is growing toward the window. This is perfectly normal if one side of the plant is getting more light. To solve this, turn the houseplant every few weeks or move it somewhere where it gets more even light.

USING GROW LIGHTS

There's no doubt that natural light is the best and cheapest option. But what to do when your home doesn't have suitable windows? For one thing, don't sit with your head in your hands, ready to give up. Artificial light will make your plant dreams possible no matter how dark and gloomy your house is.

Grow or plant lights were specifically designed to encourage plant growth. They work by producing an electromagnetic spectrum ideal for photosynthesis.

For big, green leaves, your plants will need blue wavelength light, where flowering plants need red wavelength light. Plants have no use for green wavelengths and will end up reflecting these back.

When selecting grow lights, you will have to decide which type you prefer and what your plants need. Some grow lights aren't full-spectrum and will either have just red or blue or red and blue together. A lot of people prefer full-spectrum lights not only because they're the closest match to natural light, but also because it doesn't make your house look like a bar with a pink neon glow.

The types of artificial lights available include LED lights, incandescent lights, fluorescents, and halides.

LED Lights

By far the most common grow lights available at the moment. They're especially popular because they have a low heat to brightness ratio. LED lights are usually full spectrum, but you can get lights you can program to provide different wavelengths.

Incandescent Lights

I won't use incandescent light for plants that require bright light. They are useful for plants like ferns that flourish in low-light to shady conditions. The main thing to keep in mind is that incandescent lights get hot! In fact, only 10 percent of their energy output goes toward light, and the rest is pure heat. This means you won't be able to put this light close to your plants, making them an impractical choice for high-light loving plants.

Fluorescent Lights

Here we are looking at low to medium light requirements. These lights use less energy than incandescent lights and also don't get as warm. If you're looking for a grow light for your indoor veggie patch, this is the one for you.

Halides

These lights are ideal for larger spaces since they cover more distance. Most houseplant enthusiasts won't ever need these big boys.

If you decide to go the artificial route to meet your plants' light needs, make sure you don't keep the lights on 24/7. Plants need rest too. In summer, you can aim to provide 12-16 hours of 'daylight,' while in colder months, 10-12 hours of bright light with one or two hours at a lower light setting should do.

WHAT ABOUT HUMIDITY?

Your home, as is, probably has too little moisture in the air to keep most houseplants happy. Most of the plants promoted as indoor plants come from tropical locations and thus require a more humid environment. Some of these plants even prefer humidity of 80 percent.

Since you aim to create an environment as close to the plant's natural environment as possible, you may have to utilize various methods to raise the moisture levels in the air. Winter months are especially dry due to centralized heating blowing hot air through your home. The humidity can easily fall to 20 percent, and this is far from ideal since most houseplants won't even tolerate humidity of 50 percent.

An easy and quick way to see which plants require more humidity than others (even though not foolproof) is by looking at the leaves. Plants with thin leaves usually need more moisture in the air, while those with thick or waxy leaves, or leaves covered in hair, do fine in dryer climates.

If you see curled leaves and brown tips on your plant, you have to raise the humidity.

Once you know that your plant is originally from a tropical environment where the moisture level in the air is quite high, you can start to think of ways to reproduce the ideal humidity.

Huddle Your Plants Together

In general, it is a good idea to keep plants with similar requirements together. It will make plant maintenance easier when you pass the 20-plant mark and is absolutely necessary if your collection grows to over 200! Another benefit of grouping plants is the microclimate this creates. Water moves through the plant and evaporates from the leaves.

Use a Pebble Tray

I briefly touched on pebble trays earlier on. It's a cheap way to get more moisture in the air. All you have to do is place your plant on a bed of pebbles housed in a tray that is filled with water. The only thing to watch out for when using this method is that the plant pots don't directly sit in water. It will give the plant wet feet, and this will lead to root rot.

Make sure to empty and rinse the tray each time you water your plants to avoid salt buildup and to prevent it from becoming a breeding ground for pests.

Mist Your Plants

Every good plant parent should have a mister on hand. Fill it with clean water and keep it near your plants. I suggest misting once a day, twice at the beginning of winter, when the humidity will take a quick dive. That being said, some plants detest getting water on their leaves, and it will only boost the chances of disease taking hold and ultimately kill your plants. African violet is an excellent example of a plant you should not mist; you can add any other plants with hairy or velvety leaves to the list.

Use a Humidifier

Not much explanation needed. I will say that humidifiers are godsent if you fall in love with plants from the Calathea or Marantaceae families. These plants are notorious for their hatred of dry climates. No wonder they fall under high-maintenance plants.

Shower Time

The bathroom and kitchen are the two most humid areas of the home. If your bathroom is too small to create a nook for plants to live there permanently, you can treat them to a shower every now and again.

I usually treat my high-humidity plants to a lukewarm shower once every two weeks and once a week in winter. All I do is place them in the shower for 20 seconds.

COMMON PLANT MISTAKES TO AVOID

When you're a new plant parent, you'll stress quite a bit about your plant babies. You may even fret so much that you end up doing or not doing something that will help your houseplant. As should be clear by now, many things can go wrong when you're building your indoor jungle. However, if you're sure you're doing everything mentioned in the previous sections correctly and your plant is still losing its luster, you may be making some other mistakes.

1. You're Not Pruning

Indoor plants also need a good trim once in a while. I know it is intimidating at first, and the uncertainty of where to cut and how much to cut is whirling through your mind.

It's a lot easier than you think. Grab a sharp and clean pruning tool or scissors and examine your plant. Look for any diseased, discolored, or leggy parts and snip these off. When it comes to trailing plants like Pothos, you want to cut back four to six inches. This will prompt them to push out new growth, which will lead to a bushier plant.

2. You're Fussing too Much

So many of us have done this, and the temptation to fuss is even greater when you're a new plant parent. If you find yourself poking and prodding, or worse yet, walking around with the watering can for the third time in a day, stop. Remind yourself that plants are much hardier than we think. They, in fact, can tolerate neglect better than you loving them to death.

This is particularly true during winter months when most plants go dormant. If a plant is not actively growing, you should water it less, avoid feeding, and expect the loss of some leaves. Take comfort in the fact that it's all part of a natural process.

3. You're Not Upsizing Your Plant's Pot

Repotting is crucial. I mean, how can you expect your plant to absorb nutrients and water from the soil if the roots have pushed out all the compost? A pot-bound plant can't flourish. When you repot your plant, you're giving its roots space to breathe and grow. You're also replacing old potting soil with a fresh mix full of much-needed nutrients.

One warning I have is when you upsize, don't go too big. You want to choose a pot that is only slightly larger; otherwise, you're increasing the chances of overwatering and subsequent root rot.

4. You're Not Cleaning Your Plants

Just like you dust the furniture in your house, so too should you remove dust from your plant's leaves. If you wipe a finger over a leaf and it is dusty, your plant has been suffering.

An easy way to understand why dust is harmful is by imagining the pores on your houseplant's leaves and comparing it to your skin. Whenever something clogs the pores on your skin, you can expect a pimple or something similar as a result. Clogged pores make it difficult for your skin (and a plant's leaves) to breathe. It can prevent transpiration from taking place, and this will make your plants look lackluster.

5. You Move Your Plants Around a Lot

While some plants will throw an almost immediate fit when you move them—Fiddle Leaf Fig, I'm looking at you—others will show their unhappiness over time. If your plant is content in the spot you placed it originally, leave it there. When you move a plant, it may have to get used to a new temperature, different humidity levels, and even altered airflow. This can be disruptive, and it will have to adapt to the new space, all the while experiencing stress. No doubt you'll be rewarded with a dropped leaf or two!

6. Not Checking Root Health

It's easy to get so preoccupied with what is going on above ground that we completely forget about underneath. I suggest checking the roots once a month for fast-growing plants and twice a year for the slow bloomers. All you have to do is take the plant out of its plastic pot and cut off any brown and mushy roots. If you discover that your plant is pot-bound, you can cut off any dead tips on the roots and move it to a bigger pot.

If you identify any root problems early, you are increasing your plant's chances to bounce back.

CARING FOR YOUR PLANTS IN WINTER

In winter, you will have to switch things up a little to keep your houseplants going when it is cold. Plants will look somewhat sad if left out in freezing temperatures. Most plants will go dormant during the winter—indoor plants are no exception. This is crucial for their survival when the temperature drops. However, you won't be able to see when the majority of your houseplants enter a state of minimal activity or complete inactivity; they will still look healthy on the surface. But make no mistake, your plants will definitely be in a dormant-like state in winter, and you will have to adapt your plant care needs accordingly.

Some plants may drop all their leaves and look completely dead. Don't give up on them! The roots of the plant are very much alive, and as soon as the weather turns, your plant baby will start growing again.

I own double of nearly all of my plants; half I keep inside, and the other half is to beautify my patio. In winter, however, I bring the outside plants indoors as well. They need a little extra care to adapt to being inside.

Here are some care tips to keep in mind for your houseplants when the colder months approach.

Sunshine

The light conditions in your home change with the seasons, which means you will have to move your plants to a sunnier spot. Find a window in your house that gets at least four hours of bright, indirect light. Usually, an east-facing window is ideal. Remember not to put your plants too close to the window, especially in the winter. The cold will radiate from the glass, and this will undeniably harm your plant.

Water Less

Plants that are used to being inside may take a little longer to enter an inactive state, but those you bring in from outside will go dormant as soon as they realize the light isn't as bright as what they're used to. Whatever the case may be, cutting back on watering as soon as the cold hits is advisable. Since your plants won't be using a lot of energy, they will require less water—if you continue to water at the same frequency you do in the other seasons, root rot is guaranteed.

Don't Fertilize

Plants aren't actively growing in the winter. They are using this time to strengthen their cell walls and prepare for the growing season. If you feed plants during this time, the roots will get fertilizer burn, and this will put your plant under stress, which will set it back come springtime. As soon as the temperature warms up, you can feed them with some sea kelp to kickstart their growth.

Up the Humidity

In winter, central heating systems suck up all the moisture in the air, making it much drier than during other months. So, you will have to compensate for the extra dry air by misting more or adding an extra humidifier or two. This is especially necessary if you brought any plants indoors. Outside, plants will experience fog, mist, and rain. Going from that to a very dry environment will be a huge shock—try your best to mimic the outdoor conditions they're used to. For the humidity-loving that struggle even in other seasons, I suggest creating a miniature greenhouse for them. You can use an old fish tank or build a structure and cover it with plastic. Any environment where water can evaporate and create moisture in the air will do.

Treat Leaf Spot

When the seasons change, most houseplants suffer from leaf spot. This is a condition where yellow or brown spots start to form on the edges of the leaves and progress inward. You can treat your plants by spraying them with a tonic mixed at home: four teaspoons of baking soda in a gallon of water with a few drops of dishwashing liquid.

Dust Them

There is already limited light indoors, and you don't want to reduce it even more with a layer of dust on your plant's leaves. Photosynthesis already slows down when a plant goes dormant, and you don't want it to stop entirely because your plant can't breathe. You can place smaller plants in a bathtub and lightly spray them off. The larger plants can go in the shower. Wipe the leaves with water and some dishwashing soap—this won't just clean the leaves but will also help keep the bugs at bay.

Regulate the Temperature

Remember, the idea is to mimic nature indoors. Turn up the heat during the day as it is usually warmer during this time, and at night let it drop altogether. This simulates the outdoor temperature variance and will make your plants feel at home.

Beware of Fungus Gnats

The soil will stay wetter for longer, and this is the ideal breeding ground for fungus gnats. They're annoying midge-like bugs that buzz above your houseplants. You can make sticky traps by taking adhesive tape and sticking it onto a toothpick that you poke into the ground. Alternatively, cover the soil with some cinnamon. Fungus gnats lay their eggs in the wet soil, and the cinnamon will stop them from laying their eggs in the first place.

Play Them Some Music

Okay, don't laugh. I know people think I'm crazy because I talk to my plants and play them music, but science is on my side. Plants are intelligent, even in the absence of brains. They have electrical and chemical signaling systems, which display brainy behavior and also points to the ability to remember things (Pollan, 2013). Oh, and they prefer classical music over rock and roll!

2

THE BEST INDOOR PLANTS

A s you can see, our homes may not always be the perfect environment for houseplants. Light, chiefly, is a significant issue when selecting plants. If you're not lucky enough to have a large window where light can flood in, you may have to choose houseplants that can tolerate lower light conditions.

It's possible to turn most plants into houseplants; all you need to do is duplicate their ideal environment. So, let's have a look at plants most often seen as indoor plants and their requirements.

Bright Light

Plants that require bright, yet indirect light, do well when placed in front of a north-facing window. They will receive consistent levels of light throughout the day in this spot. You just have to remember to put plants at least three feet away from the window to avoid sunburn, as well as extreme temperature fluctuations.

Bromeliads

Bromeliads add that exotic look to your indoor space. They have long-lasting, bright flowers in a variety of shapes and sizes. The leaves form a 'vase' that holds water, so you will often hear people calling them urn plants.

These plants need to be placed in a warm room with good circulation. Bromeliads like the air around them to be moisture-rich. If you don't have a humidifier, use a pebble tray to raise the humidity in the room. Direct sun will burn the plant's leaves. Pale leaves or brown tips are usually signs that there is not enough moisture in the air.

Use distilled, filtered, or rainwater and fill the central vase one inch deep—make sure the water level never drops below this. You should empty and refill the urn every two to three weeks. In summer, you can water the soil when the top inch is dry. Let the water drain completely. If your plant gets brown, soggy, or wilting leaves, it is a sign of crown or root rot caused by over-watering or poor drainage.

Most Bromeliads are epiphytic ("Epiphyte", 1998) and grow on trees, meaning they don't actually require soil to survive. Garden centers usually sell bromeliads in soil, and that's perfectly fine—you don't have to remove them.

If the flower is dying, cut it off as close to the foliage as you can with a sharp knife. These plants only flower once, but if you continue to care for it, you will be rewarded with 'pups' you can pot individually.

Urn plant (*Aechmea Fascita*), Flaming Sword (*Vriesea Splendens*), and Guzmania (*Guzmania Lingulate*) are three of the most popular Bromeliads to keep as house plants.

Anthurium

There are over 100 species in the *Anthurium* genus, but the most popular beginner-friendly plant is the Flamingo flower. This tropical plant needs warmth and humidity to grow brightly colored, wavy flowers that will last for weeks. Also, if your plant is not getting enough light, is hungry, or is planted in a pot too large for its root system, it won't flower.

With its high humidity needs, you may want to invest in a humidifier as a pebble tray or daily misting may not be enough. One way to know if there is enough moisture in the air to keep your Flaming flower happy is to look at the leaf tips. If the tips are turning brown, it means you need to raise the humidity.

Water-wise, you'll want to give it a good watering when the top of the soil feels dry. You want the soil to feel moist, not soggy. Overwatering will lead to yellowing leaves.

Spider Plant

Chlorophytum Comosum is ideal for beginners. Actually, these plants are so easy to care for, some of the more hardcore houseplant hobbyists frown on owning one. I, on the other hand, love them, especially the curly variety.

Spider plants don't have specific humidity needs—one thing less to worry about, am I right? They can tolerate the hot, dry air in our centrally heated homes, but you'll have to put up with brown leaf tips. Watering is also pretty easygoing as these plants can tolerate dryer soil better than soggy soil.

These houseplants are vigorous growers when given the right conditions. You will have to re-pot when white, fleshy roots start poking out above the soil or through the drainage holes.

When your spider plant is mature, it will produce 'plantlets' that you can cut off and share (or keep all to yourself). These plantlets grow their own roots while hanging from the mother plant, but if you cut one off without roots, just place it in water for a few days until roots appear.

Cyclamen

These plants will brighten up any room from autumn to spring. During summer, *Cyclamen Persicum* dies back and goes dormant. Don't throw it away! Place your plant outside in a dry, shaded area during summer and make sure you keep the soil slightly moist. In autumn, move the plant indoors, and as soon as you see new growth, start watering.

Watering is important in Cyclamen care. You want to keep the soil moist at all times; however, if you do forget a watering, your plant will remind you in the most dramatic way possible. Cyclamens completely collapse when dry. So much so that beginners will think there's no saving it and that they murdered yet another plant. Luckily, these plants are pretty hardy and will perk back up when given a drink.

I suggest watering Cyclamens from below as they're prone to crown rot and leaf spot when the stems or leaves get wet.

If your plant stops flowering during times you'd expect it to, check that it's not placed in a room that gets too hot. Cyclamens flower best in lower temperatures, and should it get too warm, the plant will go into early dormancy.

Dracaena

These palm-like plants are pretty easygoing. If you're erratic in your watering habits, then dragon trees are perfect for you. They will survive unpredictable watering schedules (to an extent, of course). Overwatering is not the type of erratic watering they'd easily endure. Too much water will lead to wilted leaves, or worse yet, root rot. To avoid this, take a less-is-more approach and make sure your dragon tree is planted in a pot with good drainage.

I suggest watering with distilled, filtered, or rainwater as these plants are sensitive to the chemicals in tap water.

When it comes to humidity, Dragon trees will do well placed on a pebble tray and with daily misting. They like the air to be moist, or the tips of their leaves will turn brown.

Four of the most popular Dracaena houseplants are the Dragon tree (*Dracaena fragrans*), Madagascar Dragon tree (*Dracaena marginata*), the song of India (*Dracena reflexa*), and Lucky Bamboo (*Dracaena sanderiana*).

Ficus

With dark green leaves bordering on black, or the variegated Tineke and Ruby, the rubber plant (*Ficus elastica*) is a solid favorite of houseplant lovers. It's easier to care for than the dreaded Fiddle Leaf Fig (*Ficus lyrata*) and, if you ask me, has more of a wow factor.

If your house is centrally heated, you will have to mist these plants regularly. If the air is too dry, the plant may suddenly drop its leaves. Talking about leaves, these beauties have large leaves that will need a wipe down when dusty.

Overwatering is a killer, more than ever, in the case of rubber plants. From spring to autumn, you can water when the first inch of the soil is dry, but during winter, you have to cut down on watering drastically. The leaves will curl and droop if the plant needs a drink.

Rubber plants also don't like being moved, so make sure you choose a spot where it can stay for the foreseeable future.

The weeping fig (*Ficus Benjamina*) is another popular Ficus to bring indoors. It looks more like a tree than the rubber plant, which isn't a bad thing. Who wouldn't want a tree in their house?

Palms

If I'm honest, I haven't had a lot of luck with palms. I've probably killed more palms than any other plant. But, these plants are, in fact, easy-care. You'll discover as you grow your plant collection that you may struggle with houseplants that others find easy to keep.

Palms should be kept away from radiators. They thrive in humid conditions, and that is something you should strive to mimic. If your palm is in a room that gets hot, mist regularly, or you will have a plant with dull leaves and brown tips.

If your memory is as bad as mine and you easily forget to water your plants, then palms most likely aren't for you. Although they like to dry out slightly between waterings, if you let it dry out too much, its leaves will turn yellow and drop. You'll be left with a crusty eyesore ready for the dustbin.

Palms that make good houseplants include Kentia Palm (*Howea Fosteriana*), Parlor Palm (*Chamaedorea Elegans*), and Butterfly Palm (*Dypsis Lutescens*).

Other palms, chiefly cabbage palm (*Cordyline Australis*), Ponytail Palm (*Beaucarnea Recurbata*), Yucca (*Yucca*

Elephantipes), Pygmy Date Palm (*Phoenix Roebelenii*), Lady Palm (*Rhapsis Exelsea*), and Dwarf Fan Palm (*Chamaerops Humilis*) require less watering. You can water these palms moderately whenever the top two inches of soil have dried out.

Hoya

Hoyas are all the rage at the moment. Plant hobbyists collect them like people collect stamps, but who can blame them. These plants come in different shapes and sizes and have the daintiest of blooms with a lovely smell.

Hoyas hate wet feet, so let the soil dry somewhat between watering. In winter, you can let the soil dry out completely. Although they like relatively dry soil, they do like moisture in the air. A pebble tray will work nicely.

If you want your Hoya to bloom, don't re-pot it. They look their best and are happiest when pot-bound. Once your plant starts to flower, stop misting, and don't move or re-pot as this will cause stress. Also, once the flowers are spent, you may be tempted to cut off the flowering stalks. Don't! They will re-flower at a later stage.

Some of the different varieties to look out for are Indian Rope (*Hoya Carnosa*), sweetheart plant (*Hoya Kerri*), Mathilde (*Hoya Serpens*), and my absolute favorite, Hindu rope (*Hoya Carnosa Compacta*). Of course, there are many other types of Hoya you will absolutely fall in love with.

Peace Lily

This is a staple in any plant lover's home. *Spathiphyllum* has green leaves and big white flowers. Given the right amount of light, they will flower year-round. If you have pets, especially cats, please know that the pollen falling from the flowers is very toxic to cats and can be fatal (U.S. Food & Drug Administration, 2019).

Just as Cyclamens, Peace Lilies are drama queens when they get thirsty. Sad-looking and drooping leaves will tell you that your plant needs a drink. You don't want to wait for a hissy fit every time before watering, as this puts a lot of stress on your plant. Try to water once the first inch of the soil is dry.

As with most houseplants, brown tips signify dry air. Move your plant to the bathroom or kitchen where there is more moisture in the air. It could also be due to hard water. It is best to water most plants with distilled, filtered, or rainwater.

This plant is nothing spectacular on the looks front, but hey, there's beauty in simplicity at times!

The Chinese Evergreen (*Aglaomena*) and Cast Iron Plant (*Aspidistra*) have similar care needs as the Peace Lily. If you've tried your hand at keeping a Peace Lily and have succeeded, put these two on your to-buy list.

Inch Plant

Oh boy, you'll fall in love with *Tradescantia* guaranteed. Unfussy, variegated pink or purple and green and a super-fast grower—what more can you ask for? You don't want this plant to get waterlogged, or its stems will go limp. Water when the top two inches of the soil is wet.

When some leaves lose their variegation, consider moving the plant to an even brighter spot and cut off any plain green leaves.

These plants are also easily propagated. If you want a bushier plant, cut off some stems and pop them into water. After a few days, you'll see fine, tiny roots forming. Give it a few more days and plant into the main pot.

The two most popular inch plants are Purple Heart (*Tradescantia zebrina*) and Small-Leaf Spiderwort (*Tradescantia fluminensis*).

Chinese Money Plant

I don't know of anyone who didn't immediately fall in love with *Pilea Peperomioides* when they saw it the first time. Identified by their saucer-shaped leaves growing out of the crown of the plant, Pilea is also known as the Pancake Plant or UFO Plant. They're undemanding houseplants and are easy to find since they're so famous worldwide. Pileas grow quickly, and if you give them enough light, they'll double in size without difficulty.

Just one thing about Pileas, you may see some tiny white crystals on the undersides of the leaves. At first, I was concerned and thought it was a type of pest. It turns out that they're calcium crystals, which appear on some plants and aren't detrimental to their health at all.

LOW-LIGHT/SHADE

Most houseplants do best in bright, indirect light, but some will tolerate and still push out new growth in darker areas. Keep an eye on any plants that only receive low-light; they will tell you when they need more light. If you're not sure how low is too low-light, if you can read comfortably in the space, it will do just fine for plants that love the shade.

Dumb Cane

Dieffenbachias are known for their lush foliage. That, and the fact that its poison causes temporary speech loss, hence the common name. They don't like low temperatures or drafts, so pick their spot carefully. Nothing makes these plants as miserable as cold air—not even erratic watering does as much damage as a draft.

If Dumb Canes are unhappy, they drop leaves at a remarkable speed, and you'll have nothing left in a matter of days.

Nerve Plant

This plant is known for its veined leaves. Found in the Peruvian rainforest, humidity, and heat is a must if you want to keep

Fittonia happy in your home. A room below 60°F will be too cold.

Never let this plant dry between watering, but in the same breath, don't overwater. Yellowing leaves mean you should put down the watering can. If your plant has completely collapsed, you've left it without water for too long. It will perk back up after a good drink, but letting it dry out this much more than once will inevitably lead to it dying.

The Polka Dot Plant (*Hypoestes*) has the same care needs as *Fittonia*. Both these plants are also well suited to being grown in a terrarium.

Sweetheart Plant

I know this is the second Sweetheart Plant mentioned. Well, you will soon discover that a lot of plants share similar names, which makes it very confusing. But, luckily, plants usually have more than one common name—thank goodness!

This sweetheart is also called Heartleaf Philodendron (*Philodendron Hederaceum*) because of its heart-shaped leaves. You can plant it in a hanging basket and let it vine or train it to climb up a moss pole. Heartleaf Philodendron is a fast grower when given bright light but will do perfectly fine in low-light areas. You may not see as much growth, but it will survive and green up a darker space.

You will come across a lot of Philodendrons as you research plants. It is a large genus of flowering plants. While most Philodendrons have the same basic care needs, there are some with entirely different needs.

Some Philodendrons that will do well in the same conditions as the Heartleaf include blushing Philodendron (*Philodendron Erubescens*), Rojo Congo (*Philodendron Rojo Congo*), Brasil (*Philodendron Hederaceum 'Brasil'*), Horsehead (*Philodendron Bipennifolium*), and Velvet-Leaf (*Philodendron Hederaceum Micans*).

In the following sections, I will cover houseplants that I could've included above, but I think they should get a special mention for being ridiculously easy to care for or requiring unreasonably high maintenance. Interestingly enough, easy-care plants are usually best suited to lower-light areas.

EASY-CARE HOUSEPLANTS

There's easy, and then there's this easy. Really, if only I started with one of the plants listed here. Then maybe the notion of having a black thumb would not even have crossed my mind. The two main aspects that make a plant easy-care are they can be placed in darker areas, and they won't die if you forget to water for a while or have an erratic watering schedule.

Snake Plant

There is a reason that this plant is first on the list; it's easy personified. Also known as mother-in-law's tongue (*Sansevieria Trifasciata*), it has striking sword-like leaves that are virtually indestructible. That being said, these plants are a nightmare if you're prone to overwatering. That's really the only way you can kill these tough houseplants.

You can place snake plants in bright light or low-light areas. The only thing that may happen if these plants don't get enough light is the variegated leaves may revert to all-green. But speaking from personal experience, that takes a long time. I have quite a few snake plants tucked away in dark corners, and they've yet to lose their variegation.

These plants are so chilled you can forget to water them for weeks, and they'll still look exactly the same when you finally remember to check on them. If the leaves look all wrinkly, water the plant lightly over a couple of days. You never want to shower these plants; too much water at once will lead to yellowing leaves and root rot.

Another reason why I can't get enough of sansevieria is its air-purifying capabilities. They are one of the few plants that can efficiently remove carbon dioxide and produce oxygen. They also remove Formaldehyde, Xylene, Trichloroethylene, Benzene, and Toluene from the air. I'm not going to pretend to know what all that is and does, but it sounds bad, and I don't want it in the air!

ZZ Plant

A close second to the snake plant, the *Zaioculcas Zamiifolia* will reward even the most indifferent plant parent with new growth. Overwatering, however, will kill it slowly. These plants have Rhizomes that store water, and if you water when only the first inch of the soil is dry, it will be too soon. With the ZZ, if you think it needs water, best wait another 48 hours.

If you want a lush plant, place it in bright light but avoid direct sun. Then again, if you want to add interest to a corner that doesn't get a lot of light, the ZZ will work there too.

If your ZZ drops a lot of leaves all of a sudden, it most likely is suffering from shock. If you move it from a shady area to one with bright light, best do it gradually to avoid any tragedy. No one wants a naked ZZ.

Pothos

These plants refuse to die. Whether it is trailing or climbing up a trellis, it will keep going no matter what you throw at it. They can tolerate anything except overwatering, but by now it should be clear that too much water is never a good thing.

Golden Pothos (*Epipremnum Aureum*), Marble Queen Pothos (*Epipremnum Aureum 'Marble Queen'*), Neon Pothos (*Epipremnum Pinnatum*), and Satin Pothos (*Epipremnum Pictum Argyraeus*) are all plants that will tolerate a range of light levels.

Pothos will even forgive you if you slack off on giving them water.

Helpful hint: If you want to get a vine that is not self-clinging to climb up a wall, you will have to provide an anchor point. I find that clear outdoor light clips work well to hold the stems in place without hurting the plant. They also won't ruin the wall, so they can be used if you're renting an apartment.

Swiss Cheese Plant

Also known as the delicious monster, the *Monstera Deliciosa* is a 1970s favorite. I am glad it is making a comeback because no other plant can give a room that jungle feel quite like the Monstera does.

The older the plant gets, the more fenestrations will appear on the leaves. If the plant has previously produced cut leaves and stops, it is a sign that your Monstera is unhappy. Check your watering habits and maybe move it to a brighter spot to see if the fenestrations return.

The Swiss Cheese Vine (*Monstera Obliqua*) looks like a mini Monstera and requires the same conditions.

Now, let's have a look at the difficult kids.

HIGH-MAINTENANCE HOUSEPLANTS

Just thinking about these plants makes me sigh. They are so very hard to keep alive but so beautiful you can't help but try and try again. It's torture, I tell you. The most difficult out of the lot are prayer plants. A fitting name because you will be saying prayer after prayer to keep these beauties alive. I am getting ahead of myself; I think we should discuss ferns first. They're their own kind of unmanageable.

Ferns

If I'm honest, the only fern I can keep alive is the rabbit's foot fern (*Phlebodium Aureum*). I just look at any other fern, and it dries up.

What makes ferns so difficult is their watering and humidity needs. Most ferns require constantly damp, yet not soggy, soil, and a high level of moisture in the air. Both difficult to achieve if you're a notorious under waterer who lives in a centrally-heated home.

I'm embarrassed to say that the Boston Fern (*Nephrolepis Exaltata 'Bostoniensis'*) has the highest death toll by my hands. The asparagus fern (*Asparagus Setaceus*) comes second.

Other ferns that make excellent houseplants are bird's nest fern (*Asplenium Nidus*), Silver Lady (*Blechnum Gibbum*), and the Maidenhair Fern (*Adiantum Raddianum*).

I hope you'll be luckier than me in creating the perfect conditions for Ferns to thrive. Like I said, consistently moist soil and a humid environment should do the trick!

Prayer Plants

You can put any plant that closes its leaves during the night on the naughty list. It doesn't matter if it's a Calathea, Maranta, Ctenanthe, or Stromanthe—they all spell trouble. But, they are absolutely gorgeous and well worth the grey hairs.

Prayer Plants have striking patterns on their leaves and come in colors ranging from wine-red to purple and pink. Some even have a velvety feel. They are the showstoppers of the plant world, and I suppose that gives them the right to be divas.

The two main reasons why people fail to keep Prayer Plants healthy are watering with hard water and not providing high humidity.

These plants will not tolerate tap water. You will have to use distilled or filtered water, but rainwater is best. In a pinch, you can use tap water left overnight in a container. They also want their soil to be damp at all times. Again, not soggy, but moist.

When it comes to humidity, a pebble tray with water won't be enough. When I say high humidity, I mean tropical-level high. You will have to use a humidifier, and even then, I suggest grouping all your prayer plants together to increase the moisture in the air.

If you can't fulfill their watering and humidity needs, then you'll get prayer plants with brown leaf edges that will get worse and worse until your plant loses all its leaves, and you'll lose your plant.

Some examples of prayer plants include Rose Painted Calathea (*Calathea Roseopicta*), Orbifolia (*Calathea Orbifolia*), Rattlesnake Plant (*Calathea Lancifolia*), Lemon Lime Maranta (*Maranta Leuconeura*), and Triostar (*Stromanthe Thalia*).

There are too many beautiful varieties to mention them all, but these are my top picks.

Fiddle Leaf Fig

Last but not least, and definitely not least difficult, the Fiddle Leaf Fig (*Ficus Lyrata*). This bad boy you have to put in bright light and once there, don't move it. Don't even nudge it an inch, or it'll drop a leaf! You may think I am exaggerating, and okay, I am, but this exotic tree is notoriously tricky to keep alive.

It may be perfectly happy one day, and you'll think, "Hey, I got this," and as soon as the thought has formed, a leaf will turn brown and fall off. It's as if these plants can read minds.

If you look at the care recommendations of the Fiddle Leaf Fig, it looks identical to that of Ficus Elastica, which I mentioned earlier. Don't move it, water when the top inch of soil is dry, it doesn't like dry air, and it doesn't like drafts. This is what is baffling to me. I own both and find the Elastica to be infinitely more relaxed than the Lyrata.

One thing is for sure, Fiddle Leaf Figs are enigmas.

Orchid

There are close to 28,000 species of Orchid, but what do they all have in common? They are all prima donnas of note. They need a lot of direct light and can't be placed anywhere close to drafts or where temperatures fluctuate too much. They are also very finicky about the soil they're planted in, with most Orchids preferring an aerated substance like Sphagnum Moss. This, of course, means you will have to feed it often since they won't get any nutrients from the soil.

Croton

Codiaeum Variegatum are known for their bright red, orange, and yellow leaves, but these vibrant-looking shrubs will drop a leaf at the slightest change in the environment. They absolutely loathe drafts and will let you know immediately by losing leaf after leaf. You also need to provide them with bright, indirect light most of the day, or they will lose their colorful variegation. I have mine under grow lights to make sure it maintains those vivid hues.

Venus Flytrap

Before you know it, carnivorous plants will be on your list of plants to own. That is, until after you've killed twenty and given up. *Dionaea Muscipula* and any other insect-eating plants are very difficult to care for. The soil you get them in from the garden center is usually too rich for them to handle, which already sets you up for failure if no one goes to the trouble of telling you. Carnivorous plants prefer sandy soil or peat moss—the fewer nutrients, the better. The soil should stay moist at all times, but this may be a little difficult to ensure since Venus Flytraps also like sun, which dries out the soil pretty fast. This is really a high-maintenance plant you'll have to check up on daily, or even twice a day.

Elephant Ears

It doesn't matter if they're from the Colocasia, Alocasia, or Xanthosoma family, they're going to give you a hard time. Considering that they're so breathtakingly beautiful—Alocasia Amazonica is my favorite—it is pretty heartbreaking that they probably won't survive. I've killed probably eight to date, and that number will grow since I won't give up until I can successfully keep these plants in my home! They require constant watering, but too much will kill them. With such contradictory care needs, it's no wonder they're impossible to keep happy. Bright light is best, and a daily misting won't do any harm either. Good luck with this one.

Cordyline

It's always the pretty ones that make us question if we can even call ourselves plant parents. The brighter the colors, the harder to keep alive. This family of plants is no exception with their pinks, reds, and dark greens. If you have erratic watering habits, give this family a skip. They won't tolerate it if the soil dries out even a little between watering. Also, tap water is a no-no. Use distilled even when you mist these plants.

TOXIC HOUSEPLANTS

Figure 1: It is important to know which houseplants are
toxic to your pets.

Out of the thousands and thousands of plant species in the world, only a small percentage are toxic to pets. That being said, some of the most popular houseplants do fall in the poisonous category. It is best to know which plants are deadly so that you can avoid having them in your home.

You do not want to be ignorant and spend thousands on vet trips or, worse yet, lose your beloved pet. When I first started gathering houseplants, I was uninformed of the dangers of houseplants to pets. My poor cat, who loves rubbing against and licking anything green, became too friendly with a Peace Lily. She ended up spending the following week in the animal hospital while the veterinarians frantically tried to save her life. Lucky for me, they did. I don't know how I would have lived with myself if she passed away due to my own stupidity.

The level of toxicity of plants is different. For example, eating the leaves of a specific plant will do nothing at all, while others may cause mild gastrointestinal upset, or on the extreme side, lead to kidney failure and death.

I will list some of the most popular houseplants that are also, unfortunately, bad news if you have a cat or a dog. Keep in mind that this is not an exhaustive list. I recommend you visit the American Society for the Prevention of Cruelty to Animals' website for a more extensive list (ASPCA, n.d.). There you will be able to search for a specific plant and learn if it is dangerous to pets or not.

But, for now, here are some plants you should not own if you have pets.

- Aloe vera
- Amaryllis
- Asparagus Fern
- Autumn Crocus
- Azaleas
- Cannabis

- Castor Bean
- Chinese Evergreen
- Chrysanthemum
- Cyclamen
- English Ivy
- Ivy
- Kalanchoe
- Lilies
- Oleander
- Philodendrons
- Pothos
- Rubber Tree plants
- Sago Palm
- Schefflera
- Tulip
- Yew

You can see that a lot of the houseplants I covered earlier are toxic to pets. Now, here's the problem; it's not clear if any plants are genuinely pet-friendly. According to O'Kane (2011), recommending any plants as safe is a dangerous game because we learn more and more about new toxic plants every day. For one, Gardenias have always been considered safe, but recently it was discovered that these plants do contain some poison.

Since pets, chiefly dogs, often view anything in reach as a snack, it's recommended you know what to look out for if poisoned.

Especially if a plant once purported to be harmless turns out to be quite the opposite.

Signs Your Pet Ingested a Toxic Plant

The symptoms of consuming poisonous plants can vary from mild irritation of the mouth and nose to tremors and seizures.

If your pet licks the pollen from a Lily plant, it can lead to vomiting, stomach pain, kidney damage and failure, and multiple organ failure. Cats are particularly sensitive to Lilies.

Philodendron, as you know, is an extensive genus of plants. Luckily the symptoms associated with ingesting Philodendrons are mild compared to other plants. Oral irritation, pain, and swelling of the mouth area are the most notable indications.

Other common signs of poisoning:

- Muscle tremors and seizures
- Vomiting and diarrhea containing blood
- Skin irritation
- Excessive drooling or foaming at the mouth
- Redness of ears and eyes
- Depression
- Blisters or ulcers at the mouth or on the skin
- Excessive licking
- Swelling

If you suspect Fido tucked into one of your houseplants and he is displaying any of the signs mentioned above, get your pet to a vet. Take the name of the plant as well as a picture with you. From there, your vet will know if there is an antidote or if vomiting or stomach pumping is the best route to take.

Some pet owners are fortunate in that their pets don't lick or rub up against plants. It is still a risk, but with some innovation, even those with pets can have houseplants. Place them up high or put a barrier between the plants and your pets. I am sure you will find a way.

HOW TO PROPAGATE HOUSEPLANTS

The tenacity of nature is something I've always admired—it can recover from almost anything. I can't tell you how many times I've been able to use my plants' determination to survive to my advantage. If I notice I overwatered a houseplant and the root rot is so severe that it will most likely not survive, then I take a cutting and it turns into a new healthy plant! Or, if I love a plant so much that I have to have more than one, I propagate a new baby plant. Isn't it just amazing that you can do that?

Propagating your houseplants is an inexpensive way to grow your urban jungle. Some plants like the spider plant and straw-berry begonia make it easy by growing mini-plants you can cut off. Other plants will produce pups on the side of the mother plant, which you can gently remove—the options are endless.

It's also a great way to make sure you don't lose any rare or expensive plants. Here are some tips on how to multiply your plants for next to nothing.

Cut below the node

Nodes are where the branches come out and leaves grow. This area contains a specific type of cell that can go from making shoots to roots if the conditions are right. You may see little bumps sticking out—they're raring to grow into roots.

If you want to take a cutting from such a plant, cut below the node and pop the cutting into water. Some nodes may already have grown some aerial roots, and that's even better; you can stick it straight into moist potting soil! Personally, I hardly ever have luck when I propagate straight into the soil, but other plant enthusiasts prefer that method. Let the cutting callous for a day before you add it to the water or potting soil. This prevents any rot from happening.

Start a new plant from a leaf

Other plants—Begonia and Peperomia as an example—can even be propagated from leaves. So, if you spot a fallen leaf, pick it up and check if a part of the petiole (leafstalk) is still attached. If it is, you can poke the leafstalk into moist soil and pin the leaf down with some needles. Given the right conditions, you will see a tiny plant grow from where the leaf and petiole connect.

Air layering

This method is often used on trees or tree-type houseplants like Ficus. It's perfect if you want your plant to branch out and become fuller instead of having just one stalk. You will have to be very patient as this process can take up to a year! You will start by removing the leaf where you want the new stem to be, and then proceed to make a one-inch cut through the leaf bud at a downward angle toward the shoot tip. The idea is to create a tongue you can lift and apply hormone (rooting) powder under. You will then add some moist Sphagnum moss under and over the wound and cover in plastic. You can open and check for new growth in that area, but as I said, it can take up to a year.

Imitate a greenhouse

Once you place your cuttings in soil or water, there are some things you can do to promote the growth of roots. If you can mimic greenhouse conditions, you will have the best chance of success. This means keeping an eye on the soil, air, and heat the cutting is kept in. The soil should be evenly moist and the air humid. There should be no drafts of cold air or massive temperature fluctuations. I always make a mini greenhouse by covering the container; the cutting is in with a plastic bag or a plastic cup with a hole punched in for some air circulation. In just a few weeks, you'll have a new tiny baby plant you can introduce to the rest of your plant family!

3

WHAT ABOUT SUCCULENTS?

Before we move on, people tend to use succulents and cacti interchangeably. This is incorrect, albeit not the end of the world. All cacti are succulents, but a lot of succulents are not cacti (Levine, n.d.). The way to tell them apart is through small bumps at the base of outgrowths of the plant. If you see these bumps below hairs, branches, leaves, and even flowers, you are looking at cacti. The care needs are the same, so like I said, it's not a biggy if misused.

CAN YOU KEEP SUCCULENTS INDOORS?

Growing these plants puts the 'suc' in succulents, but it's not an impossible task. The main difference between other houseplants and succulents is their light requirements. Most succulents and cacti need full sun for a big chunk of the day, while bright light will do for some. A lot of us live in apartments or houses that lack adequate lighting. Luckily, artificial lights are a cheap and efficient option to make surrounding yourself with these fleshy and plump-looking beauties an option.

The amount of water succulents need in comparison to other houseplants also differs. Where you would water plants when the first inch or two of the soil is dry, succulents like drying out completely between watering. They store water in their thick leaves and can go without a drink for quite some time. If you overwater, succulents will turn into a mushy mess and die.

The success of growing succulents indoors can be summed up in one word: neglect. I know that sounds contradictory, but I promise you if you find yourself in the mood to 'care' for your succulent, walk away. Put down the watering can, hide the fertilizer, don't pick up the pruning shears, don't do anything. If you really have to fuss, go check for mealybugs on your Calatheas. Believe me, your succulents will thank you for ignoring them.

Before I share some more succulent hints and tips, I want to tell you about one of the joys of owning these fat little plants—propagation. I know we covered propagating plants in the previous chapter, but doing it with succulents is even more satisfying—and darling. Is it not just delightful to make tiny baby plants from one mother plant? With succulents, it is easier than you may think, and instead of just roots forming, you'll be able to see a new succulent start to form on a discarded leaf!

You can either divide the plants or take a cutting. Dividing might be the best option if your succulent has little plantlets on the side of the main plant. It will also work by separating plants at the roots.

My favorite is taking pruned leaves or even those that fell off and placing them on the soil. No part of the leaf has to be underground, but you can stick the bottom part in the soil if you want. A few weeks later, you will see a teeny tiny succulent forming on the leaf. It's awe-inspiring.

It is best to let the leaf callus for two to three days before you place it in or on the soil. If you had to 'behead' a leggy succulent and you have an inch or so of the stem still attached, do the same. By giving the cutting time to callus over, you are eliminating the chances of rot. There is already water in the cutting, and you don't want the soil's moisture to be absorbed too. If the injured part where the leaf broke or was cut gets time to dry, that won't happen.

It's easy and fun, and soon you'll have shared succulents with all your neighbors.

HINTS AND TIPS TO KEEP SUCCULENTS HAPPY

You already know that light and water are the two most important aspects of growing succulents indoors. But, as with other houseplants, if you select the correct succulent to begin with, half the battle is won.

Choosing Indoor Succulents

The sad fact is that some succulents will not survive indoors, and while others may survive, they won't look too good after a while.

I know there are fabulously colored succulents out there. We're talking purple, baby blue, the deepest fiery red, and bright orange. They're so pretty, you won't be able to stop yourself from wanting to bring one home. I'm sorry to tell you that multicolored succulents need more direct sunlight than what you can give them indoors. Yes, you can use a grow light, but you will have to select one that doesn't emit too much heat.

When these colorful succulents don't get enough sun, they will reach for the light and grow lanky. If the wow-factor is what you're looking for, you'll be glad to know that appealing shapes and sizes make up for the lack of bright colors. Below are some succulents that have attention-grabbing looks, and they'll grow just fine indoors.

String of Bananas (*Curio radicans*)

This plant is too cute. With mini banana-shaped leaves spilling over the rim of the pot and dangling in the air, how could you not fall in love? A string of bananas needs filtered sunlight to grow thick and full. You can also prune it back to promote more growth.

Figure 2: The string of bananas paired with the right container can take your creativity to the next level.

String of Pearls (*Curio Rowleyanus*)

Instead of banana shapes like the Curio Radicans, you'll get a curtain of fat, round balls. One would think that the care needs of the string of pearls will be the same as the string of bananas since they look so similar. It's not. For some reason unknown to myself and most of the plant community, keeping a string of pearls alive is hit or miss.

I've killed a lot of these babies either due to overwatering or underwatering. It took me a long time to find the sweet spot with these guys.

There's also a string of dolphins with, you guessed it, dolphin-shaped leaves! The string of dolphins is easier to care for than the string of pearls.

Jade Plant (*Crassula Ovata*)

Is it a Bonsai tree or a succulent? In the strange world of plants, it's both! The Jade plant has a thick trunk and dark green leaves with a sheen to them. If this plant is happy and mature, it blooms pink or white flowers in the shape of a star. You'll want to put the Jade plant in a spot where it can get at least four hours of direct sunlight a day.

The *Crassula Ovata 'Gollum'* is a cultivar of the Jade plant I absolutely love. If you're a fan of the Shrek movies, you'll also go crazy about this succulent. The shape of the leaves looks strikingly like ogre's ears! Some types have a deep red rim on the 'ears,' and to maintain the richness of the color, sunlight is key.

Chocolate Soldier (*Kalanchoe Tomentosa*)

What a fuzzy little delight this succulent is. With silver-gray hair covering the leaves and an irregular border in brown or black, it's no surprise that this succulent is also called the panda plant.

With the help of a grow light, the chocolate soldier can bloom. But without one, no luck. The flowers are nothing to write home about; it's the woolly texture of the leaves that make this plant stand out.

For it to be happy, a few hours of direct sun is a must and bright indirect light at other times.

Burro's Tail (*Sedum Morganianum*)

Another trailing succulent, but instead of tiny bananas or pearls, you get fat leaves in colors ranging from gray-blue to gray-green. In the right conditions, each stem can grow to two feet long. That is an impressive sight to behold. Of course, it's usually the most magnificent plants that give us the hardest of times.

Burro's tail won't tolerate low-light conditions, and overwatering will lead to those chubby little leaves ending up on the ground. Much like the string of pearls, the more neglected the Burro's tail is, the easier it will adapt to indoor living. Also, place it somewhere where it won't get brushed against or knocked around. The leaves fall off easily.

Zebra Cactus (*Haworthia Fasciata*)

One of the more forgiving succulents when it comes to low-light, the Zebra cactus is beginner-friendly. It's a compact plant with horizontal white stripes. The contrast between the dark green and white makes it a standout succulent.

Since the Zebra plant has a weak root system, it is best planted in a shallow pot. Pay particular attention not to give a lot of water at once as the roots can quickly become mushy.

Aloe Vera (*Aloe Vera*)

We use Aloe Vera for so many things. The sap has some amazing medicinal properties. Wouldn't it be super cool to grow your own? You can use it to treat bite wounds, sunburn and you can even use it on your face as a mask! All you have to do to keep Aloe Vera happy is put it in a sunny spot where people won't be able to bump into the thorns on the leaves.

Hens-and-Chicks (*Sempervivum and Echeveria*)

This is one of the more feminine-looking succulents out there and is also one of the few that will survive in light shade. This succulent can't stand overwatering and will die from rot—not just root rot, the whole plant will decay!

Lithops (*Lithops*)

I don't know how I feel about Lithops. They look so weird, I'm never sure if I am fascinated or grossed out. But never mind me, they are very popular with succulent collectors for their unique looks. Easily mistaken for pebbles or rocks, they look good planted between other succulents. Give them bright light and some direct sun, and they'll be in Lithop heaven.

Christmas Cactus (*Schlumbergera x Buckleyi*)

The Christmas cactus will make an eye-catching add-on to your succulent collection. Good-looking without flowers but absolutely breathtaking with its red blooms. It's also the oddball of the succulent family as it doesn't like to dry out completely.

With the Christmas cactus, you want to water when the top two inches of the soil is dry.

Pencil Cactus (*Euphorbia Tirucalli*)

This is, in fact, a succulent-type tree that can grow up to six feet tall—even indoors! With its stubbly stems retaining tons of water, you only have to give it a drink every couple of weeks. When this plant gets damaged, you will see a white discharge. This fluid is toxic to the touch.

Pincushion Cactus (*Mammillaria Crinita*)

This is a cutie. It is a miniature cactus that won't grow taller than six inches. But vibrant blooms make up for its small size. It will add some color to your succulent collection. You don't have to water at all during winter as this tiny baby needs its sleep.

Roseum (*Sedum purium*)

Roseums require a lot of light to grow. If you can provide that, you can expect this plant to double in size in a matter of weeks. It is a low-growing succulent that produces clusters of pink flowers. You can use it as a groundcover to fill out those empty spaces between succulents potted in one container. They're also cold hardy so they can survive in temperatures most other succulents won't be able to.

Those are some of the more striking succulents that will grow well indoors. After bringing back the perfect indoor succulent, you'll have to keep a few things in mind to make certain having a succulent as a roommate isn't short-lived. I touched on watering and lightning needs somewhat, but let's delve a little deeper.

WATER NEEDS

You'll have to rein in your watering habits with these plants and quickly!

How often you water your succulents will depend on the light and growing conditions of your plant and also the size of the pot. As a rule of thumb—and this can be applied to other house-plants too—the larger the container, the more moisture is stored. The type of material the pot is made of will also affect the wetness of the soil. For example, terracotta pots dry out quicker than plastic. This is why you'll see a lot of succulent lovers using terracotta pots for their plants as the chances of plants getting waterlogged are lessened.

The time of the year also plays a role. Succulents need more water when growing, and this usually happens in early spring. During other times of the year, you can cut back on watering, especially during winter, when most succulents go into dormancy.

During winter, I have left my succulents to dry out for as long as two months. The sooner you realize that water does not equal love, particularly not to succulents, the more success you'll have.

What Is the Best Way to Water Your Succulents?

Your succulents, except those with very shallow roots, will appreciate a good drenching when completely dry. Since succulents call for less frequent watering, it makes sense to make sure the soil is completely saturated when you do water. All you have to do is water until it drains out through the openings at the bottom of the container.

A second way of watering your succulents is bottom watering. You previously learned that this method is specifically for plants that don't like getting water on their leaves. Well, most succulents fall under this category. Since their leaves are already nice and plump from the water stored inside, water sitting on top is a recipe for disaster. Not only can it trigger rot, but it can also cause leaf burn when the sunlight gets magnified through the drops, and the rays intensify.

Signs your succulents are overwatered include discoloration of bottom leaves or general translucency. Leaves will feel soft to the touch and may even burst if too much pressure is applied. The only way to save a succulent that has been drowned is to take it out of the soil, remove any dead roots, and replant it into sandy and fast-draining soil. Don't water until the soil has completely dried out.

Although underwatering is also possible, succulents will be able to bounce back easier than when overwatered. When you see the leaves of your succulent turn all wrinkly, it is finally time to get the watering can you've been yearning for!

SOIL NEEDS

The first thing on your to-do list when you bring your succulent home should be to replant it. I know you were told ordinary houseplants should be given time to get used to their new environment and not placed under unnecessary stress. But the problem with succulents is that garden centers usually use regular potting soil and not sandy or fast-draining soil.

You can buy succulent-specific soil at the garden center, or you can mix your own! All you need is sand, perlite, or pumice. Adding this to the soil will prevent compaction and leave enough space for water to flow through freely. It also helps to create pockets of air around the roots of the plant, giving it some much-needed oxygen.

Succulent specialists with years of experience have a secret ingredient they like to add to their soil: cat litter. They use it because it is lightweight, which is a plus if you want to move pots around. But, even more so, because it is porous, it sucks up the excess water from around the roots and releases it gradually. This means your succulents won't suffer from wet feet, and you won't have to see them get all mushy and die.

You can mix two parts cat litter with two parts compost for the perfect succulent soil mix. Just get a "low dust" cat litter without any chemicals added to it.

After mixing in the gritty material of your choice, wet the soil to see if the drainage is okay. If it isn't and the water stays saturated for a long time, add more gritty mix. When you're happy with your mixture, half fill a pot one to two inches larger than the container it came in with the soil. Place your succulent in the middle and use a spoon to fill the area surrounding the plant with more of your potting mix.

The critical thing to remember is no matter what container you use; it should always have drainage holes. As a last resort, you can put pebbles at the bottom of a pot without drainage holes as a type of reservoir for the water to drain to.

When you do repot a succulent or cactus with spiky bits, it is near impossible not to have a run-in with the barbs. It is especially annoying if they're tiny and get stuck under your skin. If you have some bubble wrap lying around, you can wrap it around the plant to make sure the spikes catch the plastic, not your skin.

PRUNING

If you give your succulents the optimal environment, they will soon outgrow their containers. Pruning them back into shape will make them more pleasing to the eye. Some of these guys can get out of control and end up looking like a messy mop.

The first step of pruning is to remove any dead or unsightly parts. When that is done, you will be able to see the shape the succulent has morphed into. Plan where you need to cut to get the desired shape and get at it! Use a sharp knife or a pair of clean clippers and wear gloves. Don't ever use the same tool you just used to cut off the dead leaves when shaping your succulent. If sections of your plant had a disease you didn't know about, you would now have given it to the healthy parts too. Dip the knife or clippers in alcohol before using it again.

It's best to prune your succulents just before the growing season.

OTHER THINGS TO CONSIDER

I've covered the most crucial aspects of indoor succulent care. If you follow those guidelines, your succulents will survive in your home. But there are a few other facets of caring for these plants you may want to consider.

I suggest that you rotate indoor succulents often. This makes complete sense since the plants will only be getting light from one side and will thus grow towards the light, as plants tend to do. By turning it, you will train it to grow more evenly. You can give it a quarter turn each day, or you can wait for actual signs like the plant looking askew and only then turn it.

Next up, humidity. You must be so tired of hearing about the moisture levels in the air. Well, when it comes to succulents, don't waste a second more thinking about it! Unless, of course, you live in a humid area, and by humid, I mean anything above 40 percent (in the case of succulents). Then you will have to water even more infrequently, make sure your succulent gets direct sun, and place your plant in a room with good air circulation.

Fertilizing your indoor succulents should happen only once during the growing season. Again, it's possible to get a fertilizer made specific to succulents' needs, but a regular water-soluble food will also do. Look for a nitrogen, phosphorus, and potassium ratio of 8:8:8 or 10:10:10 on the packaging and dilute to half the recommended strength.

The reason why you're only feeding once has to do with light. If you feed when days are shorter, your succulents, all high on nutrients, will keep growing and, in effect, searching for light. A leggy, awkward-looking plant will be the result of this energy boost.

You want to give your succulents room to breathe. If you plan on creating a terrarium, make sure it is an open one. If you place succulents in a closed container, it will lead to rot, and death will soon follow. It is just too moist in closed terrariums.

Figure 3: A succulent terrarium.

Succulents will need a wipe-off every now and again. House-plants don't have rain to wash away any dust. That is your job, and it is an important one. For plants to do the 'sciency' stuff like photosynthesis, they need clean leaves to absorb as much light as possible. Grab a damp cloth and gently clean away dust particles. You can mix the water with some dish soap to help keep away bugs.

Ah, bugs. Yes, unfortunately, succulents aren't immune to these little beasties. Gnats and mealybugs are the two main irritations that succulents face. Usually, pests only become a problem when you overwater or when something else is wrong, and the plant is unhappy. For some reason, if your plant is in distress, pests just know it.

If you find bugs on a succulent, quarantine it. Cross-contamination is the last thing you want. When the infected plant is away from the others, spray the soil and the succulent with Neem oil. You can also use isopropyl alcohol at 70 percent.

In summary:

- Bright light with direct sun for additional parts of the day.
- Let the soil dry completely before giving your succulent a deep watering.
- The temperature should not drop below 50 degrees Fahrenheit. Anywhere between 50 and 80 degrees Fahrenheit will be fine.
- Humidity should not go higher than 40 percent. If it does, adapt the watering schedule, give the succulent more time in direct sunlight, and place in a room with good air circulation.
- Soil should be a well-draining gritty mix.
- Check for bugs.
- Fertilize only once a year with food containing an 8:8:8 or 10:10:10 ratio.

4

RE-POTTING YOUR HOUSEPLANTS

I f your houseplants are healthy, they will outgrow their pots over time. Since strong roots are the first step to healthy plants, re-potting is more important than you think. You want your houseplant's roots to have a place to breathe and grow. You also want the soil to be chock-a-block full of nutrients the plant can absorb, and that means replenishing or replacing old soil with a fresh batch.

I know that re-potting is a scary thing to do, in particular, if you're a new plant parent. For one, I have made a few mistakes when moving my plants from one container to another. Your plants may not necessarily die if you do something wrong during the re-potting process, but they can look rather sad and pathetic for a while afterward.

Don't let your fear hold you back—the positives of re-potting houseplants outweigh the dangers.

Reasons to re-pot your indoor plants:

- New growth
- Nutrient boost
- Improved water absorption
- Disease prevention
- Plant division

WHEN IS THE BEST TIME TO RE-POT?

Most sources will advise you to re-pot during spring when plants are entering a growth stage. This does make sense since the growth will take place in both directions, so the roots will need space to sprout.

Yes, the longer days of spring means increased light and that will trigger a growth spurt. But, it is a little more complicated than that.

If your plant finds itself root-bound during other times of the year, it will be stressed out. Leaving it in that state until spring is not the kindest thing to do for your plant's health. Root-bound plants will require more water but, even more importantly, will have pushed out most of the soil from the pot and thus won't have nutrients to absorb. In that case, your plant will enter the growing season with a disadvantage, one that will be obvious above the soil.

Not all houseplants need a new pot of fresh soil as soon as spring hits. There are some other signs you should look out for before you re-pot your plants.

You Have to Water More Frequently

The more roots a plant has, the faster it will absorb water. This means the soil will dry out very quickly. So, if you find yourself holding a watering can more often than a coffee cup, consider upsizing your plant's pot.

Plant Pushing Itself Out of Its Pot

As the roots grow and grow, they will, at some point, become too numerous for the pot. As they push against the bottom and sides with no place to go, they will push the plant up and out of the container. This is definitely a sign that your houseplant needs a bigger pot.

Roots Blocking Drainage Holes

I remember one time lifting a plastic plant pot out of the decorative container it was in, and roots were dangling from the drainage holes. I knew it was time to make a plan and re-pot it; the only problem was I could not get the plant out of the pot. I had to cut the plastic carefully until the roots were free!

Plant Isn't Growing

If the roots, the foundation of the plant, don't have space to grow, how can you expect anything above the soil to get bigger? It may also be a matter of depleted soil. Have a look at the pot to determine if the plant is root-bound and needs to be potted up, or if adding fresh soil will do the trick.

Container Is Cracking

Some plants have quite robust roots, I tell you! So much so that they push against the container hard enough that the container cracks. I'm not just talking plastic here. I've seen roots break through terracotta and concrete containers.

Plant Has Been in the Same Soil for Months

There is a lot of yummy nourishment in soil, but this will become exhausted at one point or another. You can either re-pot your plant into completely fresh soil or if it is too big to remove from the container, "top dress" it. All you have to do is remove the first two to three inches of soil and replace it with a fresh batch.

WHEN NOT TO RE-POT YOUR PLANTS

We've established why and when you should re-pot, but it's also good to know when to leave a plant be.

Plant Is Flowering

On your houseplant journey, you will soon learn that plants only gift us with flowers once they are very comfortable in their new home, and the conditions are just right. You don't want to spoil this once it happens. Re-potting stresses plants out. It is known as transplant shock and is the reason why most plants will look miserable after the re-potting process. Plants will abandon any attempts to flower when they are under strain.

Plant Is Too Big

If you buy or are lucky enough to inherit your grandma's 60-year-old Bird of Paradise or something just as enormous, you won't be able to get it out of its pot without breaking either a finger or the plant. Nevertheless, large plants also need nutrients more regularly than smaller plants if you think about it. They have to maintain huge stems and large leaves, and that takes a lot of energy.

To help replenish the nourishment in the soil, you can top dress as explained earlier, instead of attempting to re-pot.

Plant Needs to Be Pot-Bound

Hoyas are good examples of plants that love sitting snugly in their pots. It is when they're root-bound that they finally push out a flower or two. Bird of paradise and the peace lily are two other examples of plants that can't concentrate on growing flowers and roots at the same time.

Plant Is Getting Too Big

You can control the size of your plant by not re-potting it. If you want to keep it the same size (give or take a few inches) because you don't have enough space, just don't re-pot it. If root development comes to a halt due to lack of space, so too will further growth above ground.

Plant Is Sick

Re-potting a plant when it is sick is only making an already bad situation worse. Unless the soil is adding to the plant's problems, i.e., it's retaining too much moisture, it's moldy, it's full of pests or fungus, etc., don't mess around with it.

Re-potting is radical and should be seen as a last resort; first, rule out any other possible causes.

WHAT SHOULD YOU DO WHEN RE-POTTING YOUR PLANTS?

If your plant is ready for an upgrade, choose a pot that is one to two inches larger than its current container. The reason is that a plant in an extra-large pot is much more likely to get overwatered and subsequently develop root rot.

A day or two before you re-pot your houseplant, give it a good drink. If a plant is watered thoroughly beforehand, you will get it out of the pot easier and with minimal damage to the roots, and the risk of transplant shock is reduced.

Below is a step-by-step guide to take some of the stress out of re-potting your houseplants.

1. Gently Pull the Plant From the Pot

This will probably be the most overwhelming part of the whole process. "What if I pull too hard and damage the roots, or injure the stems and leaves?" I hear you. The best advice I have is to work gently but put some elbow grease into it.

It will be especially hard to get a plant that's root-bound out of its current pot. If a couple of gentle tugs don't do the trick, ask a friend to help you. They can hold the pot while you tug a little harder. If the plant still doesn't budge, it is time to get your scissors. Cut down the side of the pot and gently pull it open.

2. Loosen the Root Ball

The soil surrounding the roots is probably drained of all the yummy goodness your plant needs. Gently unbind the roots and shake off any old soil. You'll also be able to have a good look at the condition of the roots once the soil has been removed. If you'd like, you can trim extra long roots, but make sure not to cut the thick roots at the base of the plant. Also chop any brown, black, or soggy roots.

If the plant was incredibly root-bound, reduce the size of the root mass by cutting the bottom and sides until there is enough wiggle room in the new container. Remember, roots packed too tightly won't effectively absorb nutrients from the soil. You would have gone to all this trouble and put your plant through stress for nothing.

3. Select the Right Container

The new pot should only be an inch or two larger than the plant's previous container. Furthermore, I can't stress this enough—use a pot with drainage holes! If that's not possible and you are forced to use one without drainage, add a layer of pebbles at the base of the container. You want to create a space for excess water to pool without being in contact with the roots.

4. Add New Potting Soil

Select potting soil that suits your plant's needs. Some plants require fast-draining soil, while others prefer soil that retains moisture but doesn't turn soggy. Fill the bottom of the pot with the soil and pack it down to remove air pockets. The bottom layer of soil is the only layer you will be compressing; doing the same to the soil surrounding the plant's roots would cause problems.

5. Add the Plant

Center your plant and fill any gaps around it with soil. I like using a spoon so as not to get dirt in the crevices of the plant's stems. You don't want to pack the soil too densely because the roots need to breathe, but you do want your plant to be secure.

6. Water

As mentioned above, you can add Limestone to peat-based soil to help neutralize the pH.

Fertilizers

Since peat-based soil doesn't contain enough nutrients, adding fertilizers is the ideal solution to help plants get all the goodies they need to grow.

You can choose between natural sources derived from mined minerals, plant materials or manures, and other animal by-products. Or, you can opt for commercially made fertilizers.

Composted wood chips

If you're looking for soil with larger than average pore sizes, adding composted wood chips will give you just that. They do rob the soil of nitrogen, so you will have to compensate by adding blood meal, alfalfa meal, or any other nitrogen-high material.

Compost

This is good stuff. Compost contains microorganisms and nutrients that will promote healthy growth. You can use leaf compost from your own backyard or buy bagged compost from garden centers. The only time I would not add compost to the soil is when you're planting seedlings. It's so rich that it will burn these young plants' roots.

Throughout *Houseplants 101*, the point has been made that much like humans, each plant has its own needs and wants to be happy. Light, water, fertilizer, and soil all depend on the type of plant. Succulents, we've learned prefer sandy, well-draining soil. But, let's leave succulents out of the equation in this section and focus on standard houseplants.

When buying, or if you're feeling adventurous, mixing soil, you have to consider adding elements that will create a light mix with small pockets for air, water, and root growth. As you water your plants, soil without adequate Perlite, Vermiculite, or sand will compact around the roots. This is unhealthy because your plant's roots need to breathe just like you do. In nature, earthworms and other bugs, as well as weather elements will prevent this from happening.

Light and fluffy is what you're looking for in a homemade potting soil.

Another option to consider is soilless mixes. By mixing peat moss, Vermiculite, and Perlite, you have a mix that absorbs moisture while resisting compaction. These mixes also completely eliminate the chances of pests or diseases as they are sterile.

There, however, are downsides. Firstly, soilless mixes dry out quickly, so you will have to be mindful of this and check your plants daily. This is not ideal if you're a busy executive who only has weekends for plant maintenance. Secondly, they contain no nutrients. You will have to add an extra step to your watering routine—mixing fertilizer—making this option more time-consuming than regular potting soil.

WHAT ABOUT SOIL-FREE HOUSEPLANTS?

I hear you going, "Huh?" But you've probably heard about hydroponics before. Well, it's not limited to herbs, vegetables, and fruit anymore.

Plants don't need soil to grow; they need water, oxygen, and nutrients. The only reason we actually use soil is for its nutrient content and because it gives some stability to plants. So, if there is a way to meet your plant's nutritional needs without soil, why not?

It's not as messy as soil, it eliminates any possibility of overwatering and underwatering, and the chances of pests and disease are significantly reduced. It also cuts plant care in half as you'll only have to replace the stale water once a month with a nutrient-rich fresh drink.

Indoor Water Garden

Growing plants in water has become so popular that a lot of plant boutique shops now sell lavish vases instead of pots for plants. What makes it more fascinating is that the plants they sell aren't limited to what we'd traditionally consider water plants. I've seen almost all the houseplants mentioned in this book sold in water and not soil—even Sansevieria, which can't even tolerate a drop of extra water when planted in soil. This speaks to the point of how resilient plants are.

This section of *Houseplant 101* will be two-fold. Firstly, I want to give you some ideas on how to create a tabletop water garden with some of your favorite houseplants. Secondly, I'm going to walk you through water gardens in the more traditional sense, but instead of focusing on creating a pond outside, we'll do it inside—fish are optional. Both of these are unique and fun ways to show off your houseplants.

TABLETOP WATER GARDEN

To build your indoor water garden, I suggest you start with cuttings propagated in water. The roots these baby plants grow are water roots, and they'll easily continue to survive in water. However, if you want to transition a soil-dwelling plant to water, it is possible. It basically comes down to you pulling the plant out of the soil, washing the roots, and putting it in water. There will be a more thorough explanation of turning your soil plants into water plants later on in this chapter, but that is the gist of it.

So, let's build on the premise that you have collected a whole garden's worth of cuttings, and you're now ready to make them a permanent feature in your home. To start, you will need a glass container. When choosing one, take the shape of the plant into consideration. You can't expect a tall plant with a deep root system such as a Chinese evergreen to fit in a shallow and wide-brimmed container. Similarly, there's no need to select a vase 12 inches deep for Satin Pothos with a superficial root system.

Of course, it doesn't have to be a clear glass container. If you prefer colored glass, your plants won't mind. Remember, house-plants should add to your home's décor—do what looks aesthetically pleasing to you. I like clear glass because I like to see what we usually can't: the roots. It is fascinating to see them grow and branch out, but it also takes away a lot of the anxiety one typically has with plants in soil. You're never quite sure if root rot is to blame for any drooping or yellowing plants, but when they grow in water, that's one less thing you have to worry about.

In fact, if the leaves of a plant growing in water turn yellow, it's usually due to light—either too much or too little. Go back to the basics if that happens and look at your plant's lighting requirements; just because they're growing in water doesn't mean their other care needs a change. Obviously, the fact that you don't have to water it is the most significant difference. I do suggest changing the water every two weeks to keep the roots healthy and prevent any algae from forming.

Also, since houseplants get all their nutrients from the soil, you will have to invest in some hydroponic fertilizer to keep your plants well-fed and happy. Buying Nitrogen, Phosphorus, and Potassium that is pre-mixed will be less of a hassle, but if you feel like playing scientist, it is possible to mix your own ratios.

This may be a good thing if you have a lot of different types of plants as the ratio differs from plant to plant. I will delve a little deeper into this later on.

I also suggest you get a pH testing kit as well as drops to bring the pH level up or down. You'd be amazed to see at what extreme ends tap water can be one day to the next. Hydrogen peroxide is also good to have as it adds some much-needed oxygen back into the water, which will enhance your plant's overall happiness. This is one of the reasons why keeping fish with a plant in a vase, or a similar small container, is not recommended. The plants will use up all the oxygen, and the fish will suffocate. If you want to add some type of aquatic decoration, use something that is made of clay. You can also include some colored rocks or beads for the roots to weave in between.

Traditional water garden—but indoors

An outdoor water garden has the ability to calm even the most high-strung person. Now, imagine if you brought that tranquility indoors—running water, the smell of flowering water plants, and even a fish or two (if your cat permits it). You can even grow herbs this way!

So, let's look at ways you can make a water garden a beautiful addition to your indoor landscape.

CONTAINERS

You're only limited by your imagination and the fact that the container should be non-porous and able to hold water. You can use anything from a glass fishbowl to a glass tea kettle, or, if big is what you're going for, buy a pre-formed pond and put it in your living room!

The only thing to keep in mind is that glass tinted red or blue will filter out the spectrums of light needed for proper plant growth.

PLANTS

Since this is the more traditional type of water garden, we'll be sticking to aquatic plants. These fall into three categories: emergent, submergent, and floaters. As you can gather, it all depends on how they grow.

Emergent plants are rooted in the soil while their leaves stay above the water. *Cyperus, Sagittaria,* and *Nymphoides* are three types of emergent plants.

Submergent plants are also rooted in soil, but they have underwater foliage. *Elodea Canadensis* and *Vallisneria Americana* are two of the most well-known examples.

Floaters, well, float! They're usually grown in soil as seedlings but are later transferred to live in water only. *Lemna, Wolffia, Trapa,* and *Pistia Stratiotes* are some floater species.

But it doesn't end there; these three categories are then divided into warm- and cold-water plants.

If you decide on using warm-water plants, you will have to provide them with permanent heat by using an aquarium heater.

Cold-water plants may make you think that you'll have to bring the water temperature down, but in actual fact, room-temperature water will do just fine. You just have to make sure that the temperature never drops below 50 degrees Fahrenheit.

SOIL

Substrate found in streams, ponds, pools, and marshes is extremely nutrient-rich. However, when you build a water garden indoors, you won't want to use soil so high in organic matter. It will smell and turn into a sludgy mess. You will focus on using chemical fertilizers for nutrients to keep the environment less fertile and thus more stable.

Use one-part soil to three parts aquarium sand (builder's sand will also work). Rinse the sand until the water runs clear to remove any dust or fine particles that will cloud the water. You can cover the soil with a layer of fine-grade aquarium gravel to prevent the substrate's unnecessary movement. Limestone or seashells will change the pH level of the water, so avoid using them.

WATER

Before adding water, remove the chlorine and fluoride with a water conditioner, water purifier, or by letting it sit uncovered for 24 hours.

When first filling the container, you'll have to work slowly—if the stream of water is too direct and fast, the planting medium will be disturbed and create a cloud of dirt in the water. You can deflect the stream against the glass or by pouring it over a stone.

Always use room-temperature water. Coldwater will shock the plants. You can even slightly warm the water in the microwave beforehand.

PLANTING TECHNIQUES

If you have a see-through container, I suggest you cultivate plants directly in the growing medium. If you're using a rock pond or another vessel you can't see through, you can lower the plant into the water while it is still in its pot. This makes it easy to rearrange without disturbing the soil at the bottom.

LIGHTING

Your indoor water garden will need to be placed where it gets between twelve to sixteen hours of light a day—unless you provide it with artificial light. If you don't want to go that route, select aquatic plants that are well-suited to shady areas. Arrowheads (*Sagittaria*), Calamus (*Acorus*), Water Clover (*Marsilea*), Elodea, and Quillwort (*Isoetes*) are good examples.

If your water garden is small enough, you can place it in a windowsill where it will get morning sun, or, on your desk under a lamp with a fluorescent bulb.

WHAT ABOUT ALGAE?

The formation of algae is a normal process, especially in newly planted gardens. As the algae multiply, they will eventually die off, and when they do, the water will become clear again. It is important that you don't replace the green water with fresh water—it will just increase the algae formation and prolong the life cycle of the algae.

I don't like using commercial algicide as too much can destroy plants. Instead, freshwater snails are an excellent addition to the garden; they will eat the algae. Just make sure to keep the number of snails in check or your filters and pumps will clog.

GENERAL TIPS

- Remove dead foliage weekly.
- Thin out floaters so that light can reach submergent plants.
- Top off the water as it evaporates.
- Fertilize regularly for success.

SEMI-HYDRO

If you're too afraid to jump all in and go the hydroponics route, there's a way to get only your feet wet, so to speak—semi-hydroponics. Semi-hydro is a technique where you grow houseplants in an inorganic medium instead of soil.

It has grown in popularity among plant parents, and those who prefer this method are affectionately known as Clayballers. It is such a fascinating topic that I'm actually writing a whole book about successfully growing soil-free plants as part of this series. But, I will contain my excitement and summarize the essential properties only. And, I will hide my optimism that you, too, will join the clayballer club.

Instead of soil, semi-hydro makes use of lightweight expanded clay aggregate or LECA for short. This clay aggregate is strong, lightweight, absorbent, and porous. The difference between true hydroponics and semi or 'passive' hydroponics is capillary action ("Capillary action," n.d.). This can be explained as a liquid's propensity to be drawn into small openings. A good example is a dry paper towel absorbing water into the tiny holes between fibers.

Through capillary action, nutrients and water at the bottom of the pot get wicked up in between the LECA. The roots, consequently, have a continuous supply of nutrients and water.

Another benefit of using LECA is the thousands of air pockets within the granules themselves, but also in the spaces between each clay ball. Your plants will never suffocate but will grow strong and healthy thanks to all the oxygen.

What do you need for a basic semi-hydro setup?

- A plastic 'inner' pot to house your plant. Make sure the pot has drainage holes at the bottom and on the sides as this is where the nutrient-rich water will enter and be wicked up to the roots.
- A decorative container with no drainage holes. You will pour the water and fertilizer mix into this container and then lower the plastic pot containing the plant into it. If the pot is opaque, you will have to lift out the inner pot weekly to see if you need to add water or not.
- Your clay balls (LECA).
- Hydroponic nutrients. You want to add nitrogen, phosphorus, and potassium to the water. It is best to

buy pre-mixed nutrients to take the guesswork out
of it.

- A pH testing kit.
- pH up and pH down drops.

Okay, I kept it short and sweet, as promised. I won't suggest semi-hydro for beginner plant parents. It can get a little overwhelming and, at times, make you feel like a mad scientist mixing so much of this with a little bit of that. When you're comfortable keeping houseplants the traditional way, you can consider transferring your plants to semi-hydro.

What, you can transfer plants planted in soil to semi-hydro and don't have to buy plants grown in water already? Since you asked, let me tell you how you'd go about doing that before we turn the page on semi-hydro.

HOW TO CONVERT PLANTS TO SEMI-HYDRO

Growing houseplants in semi-hydroponics is a relatively new practice. There really aren't any hard and fast rules, but for beginners, but there are some guidelines to help keep your plants alive. As you gain further experience, nothing is stopping you from experimenting and finding a different and maybe even more successful method.

There are a lot of plants that easily transition from soil to semi-hydro. It's as simple as rinsing all the soil from the roots and popping the plant into LECA. These easy-going plants will push out new growth as if nothing changed. In my experience, Pothos, Scindapsus, Monstera, Spider Plants, and most Philodendrons won't bat an eye when moved to LECA. The type of roots a plant has play a significant role in how quickly they adapt. The larger and thicker the roots, the more stress-free the process will be.

Plants with delicate and fibrous roots may need a little more cajoling. Peperomias, Pileas, and Marantas are good examples. It's challenging to remove soil from such thin roots without doing damage to the root system. Some plants may even lose the majority of their roots. You can imagine what a shock this will be to your plant. This is where water propagation or LECA propagation comes in handy.

When a plant's root system is injured, you can cut the roots off entirely and place the part of the stem with nodes in water. After a few weeks, new roots will have grown, and as a bonus, these will be water roots!

LECA propagation works the same as water propagation but has the added advantage of air pockets that will provide oxygen to the root zone. This combination is ideal for root growth.

Sick and struggling houseplants and those that suffer from root rot and plants with compromised root systems will need to be propagated first and then transferred to LECA.

Most plants will shed their old soil roots and grow water roots over time. Don't get a fright if you lift your plant and see mushy roots. As long as your plant looks healthy and you notice new roots growing, remind yourself that the dying off of old roots is a natural process. In time, only bright white, water roots will remain.

I suggest covering plants being propagated with a lid or Ziplock bag. Your plants will benefit from the high humidity when growing new roots. To create this mini greenhouse, you have to ensure that there is some airflow.

FERTILIZING SOIL-FREE PLANTS

Although we use the terms 'fertilize' and 'feed' interchangeably, these two actually cannot be compared. Plants get their energy (food) from light and photosynthesis, and not fertilizers. Think of fertilizer as vitamins you give your plants.

Houseplants can survive without fertilizer since the soil contains all the required nutrients; however, it is beneficial to add some extra to keep them healthy and looking good. When plants are grown outdoors, their roots can grow far and wide to seek out what they need. Potted plants don't have that luxury since their roots are confined to a container.

If you decided to go the soil-free route, fertilizing is even more critical. No soil means no nutrients, and you'll have to add fertilizer weekly or at least bi-weekly for your plants to get all the goodies they need to thrive.

To keep your plants—soil and soil-free—happy, they need 16 different elements. Carbon, hydrogen, and oxygen are required in large quantities as these are important for photosynthesis. Nitrogen, Phosphorus, and Potassium are considered primary nutrients, and you will find them in most fertilizers. In fact, since plants need a relatively large amount of these three, on fertilizer labels, you'll often see numbers like 6:12:4, which indicate the ratio of these nutrients. You may also see Magnesium, Boron, Iron, and other minor elements on the label.

Here's a breakdown of the three main elements in all fertilizers and what they're good for.

Nitrogen (N)

Fertilizers rich in nitrogen—which is always displayed as the first number out of three—will help stimulate healthy foliage. It is part of the green pigment of plants, which plays an important role in photosynthesis.

If your plant has a nitrogen deficiency, the older leaves will start to yellow, and growth will happen slowly (if at all).

Phosphorus (P)

The second number on the label—phosphorus—promotes healthy root growth and flower development. Young plants with an unestablished root system often benefit from extra phosphorus. If a plant lacks this nutrient, stems will be dark green, and foliage may have a purplish hue.

If the pH of the water or soil is not balanced, plants will not be able to use any of the phosphorus available to them.

Potassium (K)

Potassium (the last number) is such an incredible nutrient; you may be tempted to add a little too much, and you know what they say about too much of a good thing…

This nutrient promotes vigorous growth and helps plants fight diseases. It is good to give to plants before winter as it supports formation of the reserves a plant will rely on while dormant.

Suppose your plant is yellow along leaf edges or between veins. In that case, it is an indication that you need to up the potassium level.

As mentioned earlier, don't over-fertilize with potassium as it will prevent plants from absorbing other nutrients.

A fertilizer with a 30:20:20 ratio is good for most houseplants as it will promote foliage growth. If it is flowers you're after, you may consider a mix of 15:30:15—the higher phosphorus ratio will promote flowering.

Calcium, Magnesium, and Sulfur are secondary nutrients and are only required in smaller quantities. Although they're present in garden soil, you will have to add them to your watering routine if you have soil-free plants. These plants will require you to use a constant feed method.

Suppose you can't get your hands on hydroponic-specific fertilizer. In that case, you can take any water-soluble fertilizer meant for monthly use and reduce the recommended dosage by four. For example, if the label reads the fertilizer should be mixed one teaspoon per gallon, then you can use a quarter teaspoon per gallon every time you water your plants. To prevent a buildup of excess fertilizer, you should replace the water once a month.

If you don't want to use chemical fertilizers, you can take an organic approach. Liquid seaweed, Guano, or fish emulsion are some of the popular organic fertilizers you can use. Just remember that since it is natural, there will be a smell, and it usually isn't very pleasant.

In winter, when plants go dormant, you may want to cut back on how often you fertilize—instead of every watering, make it every second time you water. However, if you notice any of the above signs that your plant is lacking specific nutrients, increase the fertilization frequency again.

5

PLANT STYLING

I nterior designers have a way of crafting the inside of a home so that it's not only pleasing to the eye but comfortable to live in. A lot of the design process includes finding ways to bring the outdoors indoors. Wood furniture, stone finishes, and animal or floral print on pillows are all means to sneak nature inside. But nothing beats the advantages linked to adding living greenery to your home.

Designers never waste time thinking about IF plants should be included in their plans, and neither should you. Instead, focus on which plants will suit your space best.

Another aspect that makes houseplants great to use as home décor is the fact that you won't have to break the bank. Plants are budget-friendly additions to your home that can outlast even some furniture pieces if cared for properly. My oldest plant is 25 years old! It was my mom's, but she decided to give it to me when I first moved into my own apartment. She knew that adding just one plant would make me feel immediately at home in a strange place. That, and I would have something if not someone to talk (and sing) to.

Back then, I figured out that caring for another living thing, even if just a potted plant, made me happy. Connecting to nature when you're in an urban structure should never be taken for granted.

But, owning houseplants can be about much more than just placing a plant here or there. If you put your mind to it, you can Fung Shui your house into a peaceful indoor forest. Or, style your plants to accentuate the elegance you want to depict through your design aesthetic.

Use plants to soften the hard edges of a corner or hide some unsightly aspects. Some plaster came off the wall, and you don't have the time or money to fix it now? Don't worry, hang a plant in front of it.

A clever idea is to turn plants into furniture! Don't buy a room divider; instead, skillfully stack and arrange plants vertically. You can hang planters from the ceiling all the way to the ground to create a living wall or build an installation specifically meant to hold plants. This is an inventive way of merging fun and functionality while keeping it stylish.

With a range of sizes, colors, and textures to choose from, plants are versatile décor accessories.

You can use houseplants with different textures strategically to emphasize a more masculine or feminine space. Snake plants, for one, look great in geometric areas generally assigned to more masculine designs. I like the aesthetic of a dark grey wall with angular plants in white pots adding contrast.

Rooms meant for the feminine among us usually have more curves, so you can add to that style by bringing in plants with soft edges. The Calathea Orbifolia is an excellent example of a houseplant that will fit into a more feminine space.

Then again, it is sometimes pleasing to the eye when you juxtapose hard edges with soft textures. Think of a Dracaena in a colorful patterned pot against the backdrop of a white faux fur throw. The mix of the spiky leaves with the soft throw somehow brings balance to a room, while the patterned pot adds some playfulness.

Take into account the different sizes of houseplants, and it will be a struggle for you to name any design item that is more versatile than houseplants. You can cheer up a dull desk with a tiny plant in a cute pot or make a large indoor tree the focal point of a room. The options are endless.

Plants can act as an organic layer to emphasize your home's or even an apartment's architecture. With some thought and planning, you can bring a room to life with your houseplants.

TIPS TO STYLE YOUR HOUSEPLANTS LIKE A PROFESSIONAL

In the beginning, figuring out how to include houseplants in your décor may be somewhat challenging. Although bringing plants indoors is a great way to introduce color and texture, you want everything to look thought out and intentional.

There is no manual saying do this and don't do that, but by following some guidelines, you will feel less overwhelmed by it all.

Keep It Simple or Don't

If you consider yourself somewhat of a minimalist, pairing a large plant with a solid-colored pot and placing it in a corner may be all you need to liven up the room. Aim for plants with attractive foliage like the Fiddle Leaf Fig with its enormous, teardrop-shaped leaves. Large is the keyword here; too small and your plant will look lost and out of place, and this will tilt the balance of the whole room toward the unsightly end.

Another worthwhile idea for minimalists is to make use of unused entryway space. Placing a large tree there will make it feel like you're coming home to a friendly face and a warm embrace after a long day's work.

You can either plant the tree in a pot. Or, if you want to trick the eye, choose a smaller tree and build a raised garden bed indoors. Add some pebbles, and it will seem as if the house was built around the tree! But the tree should not be too small; you still want it to claim its space and stand out.

Then there are the houseplant collectors whose aim it is to turn their indoor spaces into a jungle. I am unashamedly one of those plant parents who believe more is more. But, that doesn't mean my house looks like a cluttered mess.

If you want to surround yourself with green, you can still do it stylishly and in an orderly manner. For one, I have various plant corners throughout my home. Each with a specific design aesthetic to fit the room. The plants in the kitchen are in white pots to offset the black marble countertops while blending in with the white of the cupboards. I've limited the plants to different shades of green.

Make a bold statement by grouping plants together. You don't have to band together green with green and color with color. Depending on your style, mixing it up will work wonderfully. Select plants of assorted colors, sizes, heights, and textures and be bold with your design.

The bottom line is, you won't look at a home and say, "Oh no, I don't like it. There are too many plants". Somehow, plants don't ever make a room feel cluttered. It's as if they have this magical ability to breathe life into any space.

Choose Plants, Not Furniture

Okay, that might sound a little extreme, but how often have you pushed a lone chair into a corner that looks bare? It's not like anything will ever use the chair; it's there as a prop, nothing more. Instead of going that route, why not select a few plants of varying heights? Or, even just one big statement plant? Really, any plant will give the corner more depth than a lonely old chair. If you have to have a chair in that space, consider placing a tall plant behind it. It makes a lovely backdrop to your furniture.

Another top tip is to place plants in front of mirrors. It multiplies the green while adding depth to the room.

Switch It Up

Snake plants are versatile, but what about going for the unexpected? A dwarf fruit tree in your living room will surprise and delight all your visitors. Lemon trees are my favorite; that pop of yellow will brighten up any room.

Figure 4: Air plants come in shapes and sizes that make them attractive additions to any plant collection.

Air plants (*Tillandsia*) are also something different to consider. They come in unique shapes, sizes, and colors. You can group them on a table, place them in a glass container, or hang them from one of the many attractive geometric air plant hangers that are available. I've even seen some houseplant hobbyists create the most delightful wall art using air plants.

Air plants are easy-care, requiring only a thorough soaking once a week. If you see the leaf edges roll up, it means they are thirsty. To stop this from happening too often, mist them every second day in between watering.

You also need to feed your air plants if you want to get them as fat and plump as the ones you see on your social media pages! Since standard houseplant fertilizer doesn't have the right balance of nutrients specific to epiphytic plants, you will need to look for a specialist product. Your garden center will most likely stock food formulated for *Tillandsia*.

If you have a pond or freshwater aquarium, you can use water from there to mist your air plants—it contains enough of the right kind of nutrients to keep these plants happy. Actually, they're more than plants, they're living sculptures, and they make for interesting conversation starters!

Add a Terrarium

A world within a world. You can opt for a more simplistic, low-maintenance terrarium, maybe an open one with a few succulents and pebbles. Or, you can go all out and convert an unused fish tank into a mini greenhouse where you can keep moisture-loving plants. Closed terrariums are essentially self-watering as the moisture released trickles down the glass and back into the soil.

Don't Forget About the Ceiling

Hanging planters or beautifully intricate macramé are ideal for displaying some of your favorite trailing plants. Of course, if you run out of space on the floor, you have no choice but to make use of the ceiling. You can hang them in strategic places to create curtains of foliage throughout your home. Just make sure that they are getting enough light.

Containers Are Key

Choosing the perfect pot for your plant is probably the easiest way to make a statement. With colors, patterns, and textures to choose from, you won't be hard-pressed to find one that perfectly fits your décor. The secret is to pick a pot that enhances your plant's beauty.

You may think that any pot can be paired with any plant, but you would be wrong. For example, putting a pink plant in a pink pot is not a good idea. The colors will fuse together, and you will spoil the plant's magnificence.

By grouping plants in pots of complementary colors together, you can effortlessly create a focal point in any room. Planters that tie together will make the room look like a top designer came for a visit. Vary the sizes to make it visually more satisfying to look at. Also, keep in mind that everything is better in odd numbers. Grouping three or five plants together will be a hit!

Another thing to keep in mind is the size of the plant. You don't want to pair a thin-stemmed plant with some height with a narrow pot. Firstly, think about whether it will be practical? You don't want your plant to be too heavy for your pot and topple over. It's best to select a pot that will be heavy enough to offer support while also balancing out the plant's height.

It may also be helpful if you place oversized plants on wheels. That way you'll be able to move the plant around as the seasons and the lighting conditions in your home change. All you need is a slab of stone, or even wood will do if the plant is not too heavy. Attach four wheels, and your life just becomes so much easier.

For more sizable containers, you don't have to feel pressured to find a plant big enough to fit in them. I have a thing about using large containers to plant different plants in. No rule says each plant should have an individual pot. The only restriction is grouping plants with different watering needs together in one planter. You can imagine what havoc it would be if you planted ferns in the same pot as succulents.

To the more creative among us, don't be afraid to use unusual objects as planters. A wooden box that is just lying around can quickly turn into a rustic container for your houseplants. Let your imagination go wild.

Combine Plants with Art

You want your home to tell a story. If you're like me and end up creating various plant corners throughout your home, add a piece of art to each section. You can keep to the plant theme and hang a Monstera Leaf painting, or you can bring in contrasting colors with your selected art pieces.

A statue or some other accessories like a candle or two will add to the area's cohesiveness.

Alternatively, you can turn your plants into art. There are gorgeous vertical planters on the market you can use to spruce up a bare wall. Add various plants, and you'll have a living work of art.

High and Low

You don't want all your plants to be placed on the ground.

There are a variety of plant stands for you to choose from. You can even get space-saving stands designed specifically to maximize corner space. These stands frequently have different levels to accommodate more plants. Something that is ideal as it helps the eye hop from one level to another. But, in its totality, it provides a focal point, especially when you're comfortably seated on a couch. There's no denying that placing plants at different heights creates visual interest.

If you don't have space for a plant stand, use bookshelves, a trailing plant on the top shelf, a smallish plant in the middle, and a larger plant on the ground.

Shelves Are for Plants

Any space where you can place a plant is where a plant belongs —of course, bearing in mind the plant's light requirements. There's a reason why a 'shelfie' is a thing. Plant parents just love using bookcases and shelving to create exciting displays of their houseplants. Adding living elements between books and knick-knacks just adds something comforting to a room.

Let Plants Be Plants

Always keep the type of plants in mind when you decorate a specific area of the house. If you place a vining plant like Golden Pothos on the ground, there isn't much space for it to do what it does—trail. However, if you put it on top of a shelf, there will be more than enough space for the vines to drape down.

The same goes for larger varieties of Philodendron like the Hastatum, also commonly known as p. Silver Sword. This plant gets big and needs space to grow vertically and horizontally. If you squash this beauty into a corner, you're not doing the plant any justice. The large silver-green leaves won't have room to grow, and the new leaves will suffer damage from being pressed up against the wall.

Allow your plants to do what they do best—grow.

DIY HOUSEPLANT CONTAINER DECORATING TIPS

With a glue gun, a can of paint, and some imagination, you can take the most boring pot and give it a facelift. Or, if you're adventurous, take any ordinary object and turn it into a planter. If you have kids, you can even rope them in to help you and turn it into some fun-filled quality time. As a bonus, you may spark a love for plants in your little ones.

I am a big believer in upcycling as a way to help the planet. Instead of useless household items ending up in a landfill, you can transform them into a lovely new container for your plants. Drainage is the only requirement.

I've seen everything from an old wheelbarrow to even a toilet transformed into planters. These work best for outside areas, but an old kettle or even a rusty old colander can make out of the ordinary pots for your houseplants.

Before we get to the wild and extra creative planters, I want to share with you three quick and easy ideas to breathe some life into a boring old pot.

Spruce Up a Pot Quick and Easy

The sad truth is that modern pots are expensive. Why this is, I'm not sure. Maybe manufacturers are trying to cash in on the plant craze taking the world by storm. After all, plants are the new pets.

When you have a budget to think of, you are forced to take matters into your own hands and get creative! It's fun to add your personal touch to some decorative pieces you'll be using in and around your home. So, gather all your cheap plant pots, grab some tape, scissors, paint, brushes, and tarp. You'll be turning your pots into stylish, expensive-looking masterpieces worthy of your houseplants.

Take your first pot and use your tape to block out a pattern of your liking. Vertical or horizontal lines of varying thickness, zig-zag shapes, triangles, or waves, it doesn't matter. Once done with your patterns, you can paint the whole pot with a brush, or use spray paint to save time. Choose a color that won't clash with the original color of the pot. Remember, when you peel off the tape, that color will show.

Waiting for the paint to dry is torture. I'm not one for delayed gratification, and it took all my resolve not to remove the tape while the paint was still wet. You will ruin the pot if you touch it when still wet, even if just slightly. After I painted the pot, I put it somewhere where I couldn't see it for the next 24 hours. That way, I would not be tempted to rush the process. You can't touch what you can't see, right?

Once dry, you can peel off the tape and be amazed at your artistic brilliance. If you're not happy with the look, you can add more tape in areas where you feel it's looking a little too blah. You can also add some dots in between the lines or turn one of the other pots into a polka dot planter! I am particularly fond of a polka dot pattern on planters. There's something so playful about it, yet it still looks stylish.

In 10 to 15 minutes (minus the drying time), you created a planter that you would typically pay a premium price for. Well done!

The next DIY project may take a little longer, but it is a solid favorite of mine. In addition to your pot, you will need a glue gun and hessian rope. You can use any other rope, but I personally like the rustic feel of hessian.

Start by gluing one end of the rope to the pot. Now, rotate the pot in your hand, winding the rope up in layers as you go. Make sure to put a glob of glue on each layer to make certain it doesn't slip off when turned upright. Continue doing this until you reach the top of the container. When done, it should look like a basket and not a pot!

You could also paint planters with chalkboard paint. This works very well for herb gardens, especially in the beginning when you're still struggling to tell the different herbs apart.

Okay, you may think I'm absolutely off my rocker for suggesting this, but hear me out. You know about the monster that lives in laundry baskets, right? The one who likes to eat socks but never two of the same kind? Well, I am suggesting that you use your mate-less socks to cover planters. Succulents or tiny plants in pots wearing bright socks with funky patterns will work well in a craft room or even a kid's room.

Let's Get Creative

It is time for the imaginative and daring plant parents to come out and play. Say it with me: "If you think out of the box, anything can be a planter."

All you have to do is to rummage through cupboards and storage containers to find something to turn into a houseplant container. Believe me or not, I have seen people use even clothing as planters! With a bag of cement, you can go wild.

Let's have a look at various items you can upcycle into a planter.

- Old tea kettle
- Various tins
- Jugs
- Used food cans
- Bowls
- Colanders
- Chest of drawers
- Children's toys
- Shoes and boots
- Birdcage
- Pallets
- Cups and saucers

Everything listed above and anything else you think is planter-worthy will most likely just need a good clean and some paint to revitalize it. Making sure the container has satisfactory drainage is super important as well. But that's nothing a drill or even a screwdriver and some elbow grease can't fix, am I right?

Paint mason jars in colors matching the interior of your home and hang them in front of a window in place of curtains. Succulents will love the light, and since they don't have extensive root systems, they'll be perfectly happy in a container a bit on the smaller side.

If you think yourself amusing, why not display your personality on the planters. Turn plain pots into face pots by wrapping and gluing mugshots of all of your family members on the container. Crop the photo so that the plant's foliage will end up looking like your hair. It's quirky and fun and will bring a smile to anyone's face.

Plants breathe life into interiors, yet they are more than just decorations. They might as well be residents. They have the ability to turn a house into a home. Give them space and the trimmings they need, and they will make magic happen.

6

BONUS - EDIBLE PLANTS TO GROW INDOORS

Why not put your newly obtained green thumb to work and grow your own veggies, fruits, herbs, and even edible flowers indoors? You can dedicate your kitchen's windowsill to the project or go wild and use a whole room. Growing your own food to eat is not only satisfying, but it is also good for you and the environment (Gomes et al., 2017). I have several books on this subject in this series.

Planting your own edible plants has the added benefit of you knowing exactly where your food comes from. It's no lie that food labels can sometimes be deceptive.

If you live in an apartment, don't let your lack of space put you off of growing an edible garden. It may be challenging, but it is not impossible. You don't have to be a farmer; resourcefulness is all you need.

There are various fruits, veggies, and edible flowers that will grow in containers without any difficulty—when given the right conditions. Just like houseplants, sun, soil, water, and environmental conditions will affect your success rate. You also have to consider how much space specific edible plants will need to grow.

It's a piece of cake, wait, make that cake with homegrown carrots!

Before we get to the how let's backtrack to sustainable living and lessening your carbon footprint.

ENVIRONMENTAL BENEFITS OF GROWING YOUR OWN FOOD

Sustainable living is a hot topic. Going green is the best way to break off our relationship with buying fresh foods from a shop. You may be wondering why you'd have to give up the convenience of shopping for your food.

The answer has many sides, but if you care for the planet, reducing the negative impact mass-produced foods have on the environment should be a top consideration. Fresh food from commercial farmers has to travel miles before reaching the store. Not only does this have an effect on the freshness and flavor of the fruits and vegetables, but it also contributes to carbon emissions and general pollution in the atmosphere.

The most serious danger associated with burning fossil fuel is the rise of the planet's average surface temperature. The phenomenon of global warming is permanent, and the related consequences spell out a bleak future for the coming generations.

Add to that the fact that the packaging – usually man-made plastics—ends up in the ocean and is endangering marine life. Going green suddenly looks like the humane thing to do.

Apart from the risk mass-produced foods have on the planet, the carcinogenic pesticides and fertilizers used are harmful to your body (Dich et al., 1997).

Herbicides, insecticide, fungicide, and soil fumigants aren't only on store-bought fruit and veg; these toxic chemicals also seep into our drinking water. Studies have shown that ingesting pesticides is markedly more dangerous to children, even before birth. But, you may be saying to yourself, "I buy organic." Although buying from organic farmers is better, they unfortunately still have to make use of pesticides. The bottom line is, the larger the operation, the greater the need for chemicals. If you grow your own fruit and veggies on a small scale, you get to decide what to use on your plants and what to put into the soil.

Don't get me wrong, buying locally grown food is a step in the right direction, but if you build your own edible indoor garden, you're sprinting toward better health and helping the planet too.

28 OF THE BEST EDIBLE PLANTS TO GROW INDOORS

You may be in awe of all the fruits, vegetables, and edible flowers you can grow indoors. Next time you make homemade pizza, you can harvest most of the staple plant ingredients from your own garden!

Avocados

I know you may be tempted to try your hand at growing an avocado tree from a pit. It may be a new test of your green thumb's abilities, but a plant grown from a pit will very rarely carry fruit. Ideally, you're looking for a grafted dwarf tree.

To successfully grow these trees in containers indoors, you will have to give it adequate light. Once the plant starts to produce leaves, pinch off some growth to get the tree to grow stronger and bushier. If you live in a centrally heated home, your avocado plant will not carry fruit. These plants require colder temperatures at night to force blooming. Even still, it may take years for the tree to grow mature enough to produce fruit.

Lemons

Standard trees are much too large to grow indoors, so you will have to pick out a dwarf variety. Lemon trees need up to six hours of direct light a day. If you don't have a spot in your home where that is possible, consider providing another light source.

Your lemon tree won't die if it doesn't receive enough light, but it won't flower or produce fruit.

Mandarin oranges

You don't want to place orange trees near vents that will dry out the air. Orange trees need fresh air, but it has to be humid. If the moisture levels are low in your home, consider using a humidifier.

I suggest placing the container on wheels to make it possible to move the tree outside during summertime. This will turn the fruit deliciously sweet.

Tomatoes

Choosing the correct variety of tomato is your ticket to success. Small and upright types like red Robin are ideal. You can also get tomato plants that vine. If you train these to arch over door frames or around windows, you'll have beautiful green foliage with pops of color.

Carrots

The depth of the container is key when growing carrots; the deeper, the larger the carrots. Be sure to harvest the carrots by pulling them out of the soil. If you dig around in the dirt feeling for carrots, you'll disturb the roots of the younger carrots, and you may end up with deformities.

If you want extra sweet carrots, eat them when they're tiny and immature.

Lettuce

Lettuce isn't as easygoing as other edible plants. You will need to pay a little more attention to them. You want young plants to look green and full-bodied. If your plant is yellow and leggy, you need to move it to a brighter spot.

Microgreens

Microgreens are tiny versions of vegetables. It is a sprouted seed given a little more time to grow but not enough time to fully mature. They're easy to grow in containers indoors, and you can bunch them snugly since they won't reach full-size. You'll be eating them way before then!

Scallions

This is one of the plants that I love growing because you use scraps to start a new plant. All you do is push the white ends into the soil or place it in water. Soon, you'll see new growth. I find that growing scallions in water goes a little faster than soil.

Placing the plant somewhere where it can get bright light for six hours a day is not a hard thing to ask. They can tolerate lower light conditions, but it will take much longer for them to grow.

Chives

Chives don't require any fussing. It's a case of putting the plant in the soil and letting it do its thing. Since chives don't have massive roots, you can grow them in shallow containers.

Basil

Basil wants well-draining, nutrient-rich soil. Water stress is something you should absolutely avoid, so no overwatering and underwatering. Keep the soil moist but not soggy.

Cilantro

Cilantro prefers colder climates. As soon as the temperature rises to above 85 degrees Fahrenheit, it will start bolting. This is the plant's reproductive mode, and its leaves will thin out, and all the flavor will be lost. Other than that, cilantro is a forgiving plant, so don't stress too much.

Ginger

Ginger is a slow starter; however, you can speed up the process by placing it in a terrarium. Once it takes and starts to grow, keep in mind that it's a hungry little plant and equally, if not more, thirsty.

On top of that, you will need to give it a lot of room to grow. It will take a piece no larger than your thumb just six months to fill a 2-gallon pot.

Mint

Much like basil, watering is an issue; too little or too much, and you'll have no mint for your Mojito. Keep it evenly moist and mist it daily to raise the humidity in the air. If you want your plant to have a uniform look, rotate it every four days.

Rosemary

Not even a bright window will do for this herb. You will have to place it somewhere it can get full sun. If that is impossible, it is best to get your rosemary used to lower light areas slowly. To do this, start by moving the plant from full sun to shadier areas for only a few hours a day. Progressively increase the time in the shade, and your plant should be more capable of handling lower light when moved indoors.

Green beans

Choose a bush bean variety when planting beans indoors. They are smaller and will do better in containers. Place the plant in full sun or a space, most likely near a window, where it gets at least six hours of bright light a day.

Potatoes

Potatoes are super easy to grow. The container size is the only thing to worry about; a 2.5-gallon capacity is the sweet spot. You can use a bucket, a pot, or a used fertilizer bag.

Kale

Kale tastes better after being exposed to extreme cold. So, if you keep your home warm and toasty, this is not a vegetable I recommend you grow indoors. You're looking at a daytime temperature of between 60 and 65 degrees Fahrenheit and 50 degrees at night. To achieve these temperatures, you can place your kale in a windowsill, and that way you won't have to give up your comfort for a plate of more flavorful kale.

Mushrooms

Cool, dark, and damp. Those are the only three aspects you'll need to get your own mushroom farm going. A basement is an ideal place, but if you lack this underground space, an unused closet will do nicely.

Bell peppers

These brightly colored vegetables are very sensitive to air quality. If there is an excessive amount of pollution in the air, cigarette smoke, for example, the plant will get damaged. Suppose that is not an issue in your home. In that case, pepper plants can be successfully grown indoors as long as the environment is warm, and the plant receives sufficient light.

Parsley

Give Parsley ample light and plentiful water, and that is it. This herb is low maintenance. If you see your plant is growing spindly and sparser by the day, it is a sign that it needs more light.

Nasturtiums

If you grow this edible flower indoors where it does not get a lot of light, the flavor will be milder. Should it get full sun, you can expect a strong peppery taste.

Marigolds

This is a great edible flower to brighten up your kitchen windowsill. They're hardy and come in different shapes and sizes. You can plant the taller varieties like crackerjack marigold in the back and the more compact types like dwarf French marigold in the front. The colors will add a lively country feel to your edible indoor garden.

Calendula

This plant can adapt to most environments; it can even tolerate poor soil. If you want it to produce blooms, fertile soil is the way to go. You can put it where it gets full sun or in partial shade.

Hyssop

This herb will grow up to two feet if not pruned regularly. It is tolerant of different environments. Because this plant is so easy-going, it is just right for the indoors. It will even forgive you if you forget to give it a drink now and again.

Honeysuckle

This is a pretty large plant to move indoors. That is the only drawback of adding this plant to your edible indoor garden. It can grow up to 20 feet tall and just as wide. But, if you have the space and time to keep this aggressive grower in check, go for it! Just remember to give it substantial support to hold up its vines.

Chamomile

If your nerves are shot because you just can't crack a specific houseplant's care needs, you can harvest some chamomile to relax. I just love growing this plant indoors. It has the daintiest flowers, and the smell is refreshing yet calming.

It's easy to grow, especially if your house only gets bright light for parts of the day. Chamomile needs only four hours of bright light a day, so keep it near a south-facing window. Its soil should be moist but not soggy.

Broccoli

This veggie likes cooler temperatures even though it enjoys sunbathing for at least six hours a day. Plant broccoli in nothing smaller than a 3-gallon container and leave at least one and a half inches around each plant for it to grow into.

Cauliflower

Cauliflower needs soil that retains moisture but doesn't become waterlogged. You can add some bark, vermiculite, or perlite to the potting mix to make sure the soil is well-draining.

I'd avoid using regular garden soil as it will compact more and more after each watering, and no air will be able to reach the roots. Suffocating roots means a slow death for your cauliflower.

You should not limit yourself to this list. If you love a specific fruit, vegetable, herb, or edible flower that I didn't mention above, do some research. It would be great if you could add as many of your favorites as you can to your indoor garden. It will definitely make a dent in your grocery budget.

Now that you know what you can plant in your edible indoor garden, you must be wondering what type of containers will do the trick.

CONTAINER IDEAS

Earlier, we had a look at some strange and creative planters. However, just because you're growing fruits and vegetables, it doesn't mean that you can't get resourceful. As always, keep drainage in mind; edible plants also aren't very fond of having wet feet.

Here are the best space-saving ways to grow fruits and veggies in your home.

Pots and Other Planters

What I like most about using pots is that if you move, you can take your plants with you! Since pots come in different sizes, you can make sure you select a container big enough for a specific plant's needs. Fruits and vegetables need a little more space to grow than normal houseplants. On the other hand, herbs mostly have small root systems and will do well in smaller pots. Not only that, but you'll also be able to control the size of your plant if you limit the space where the roots can grow.

Plastic pots and planters are cheap and lightweight. You can even upcycle plastic bottles into planters for smaller plants. Terracotta pots are heavier but add more of a design element to the room.

An aged terracotta pot with a citrus tree planted in it immediately transports you to a tiny village in Italy. You can patina your terracotta pots if you're impatient and want to give a new pot more character. One way is to soak the pot in salt water, but that method takes a little too long for my liking. I usually grab a dry brush, dip it into some white paint and brush on the 'patina.'

Cans, Tins, and Jars

Old food cans, biscuit tins, and glass jars are great for housing herbs. Wash the empty food cans, paint them in colors that fit your kitchen's theme, and use them to grow some sweet-smelling herbs. They don't take up a lot of space, so a windowsill is an ideal spot to place these colorful containers. Permitted it is sunny enough, of course.

Mason jars, vintage jugs, or any other glass containers look lovely with an assortment of colored root vegetables or herbs planted in them. In addition, you won't need to use any counter space. You can tie a rope around the necks of the bottles and hang them on a wall or in front of a window. Think of it as a functional work of art!

Jars are also useful for sprouting seeds. Soak seeds, beans, or grains in a glass jar and cover with a cheesecloth or muslin. Drain and refill the water twice a day, and after a while, shoots will appear. These sprouts add crunch to a salad and nutrition to your body.

Hanging Edible Garden

If you have a bare wall that gets ample light and even some sun and you're out of ideas on how to make it work for you, turn it into a vertical garden. Wall gardens are all the rage, and it is understandable why. It is an aesthetically pleasing way of greening a specific space. But, an edible wall garden takes it a step further—it gives it a function too.

Use a wooden pallet or other containers filled with herbs and edible flowers and hang it against the wall. It will immediately add a green wow-factor to the room and beautify the space. If you're lucky, you'll be able to hang it in reach for when you're busy cooking up something delicious.

If you use planters to create the hanging edible garden, place them in an exciting pattern to kick the novelty up a notch.

ENSURING YOUR SUCCESS

There are some handy tips you have to keep in mind to guarantee your success.

Before you get started, let's go shopping. You'll need pots or containers of your choosing, but remember the drainage holes and keep the plant's size in mind. Grab some potting soil suited to your plants' needs. You may want to add perlite into the store-bought potting mix to safeguard against soggy, waterlogged soil. Select your fruit and vegetables, herbs, and edible flowers and get potting. I recommend choosing different plants and mixing them together. It will turn your edible indoor garden into an attention-grabbing focal point while also increasing the air's moisture.

Veggies will need at least four to six hours of sunlight a day, and fruits double that. Herbs and edible flowers can do with less sunshine. Edible plants also like a warm environment, so keep that in mind when selecting where to place your indoor garden.

If you don't have a sunny window for your indoor garden, get yourself some grow lights. They're not expensive and will prevent you from having to wait weeks to months before you can enjoy your harvest.

Since edible fruit and vegetables, herbs and flowers are plants; you can apply the same watering rule to them as you would your ordinary houseplants. Less is more. The watering needs of all the plants won't be the same; group plants together according to how thirsty they are.

You can feed your plants earthworm casting tea or other organic fertilizers to boost growth and harvests.

Start small, as soon as you feel you know what you're doing, then you can experiment with other edible plants. That is the only way you will find out which plants grow well in your home and go well in your mouth. The height of your ceiling only limits you!

CONCLUSION

The revival of the houseplant craze of the 80s should be celebrated. It doesn't matter if you're young or old if you live in America or Africa; plants speak a universal language. Caring for houseplants not only feeds the soul, but it has a more tangible impact on you physically and psychologically.

If you're after increased productivity and better cognitive health, or if you're looking for a mood-booster that will also reduce stress—think plants. And breathing cleaner air is nothing to scoff at either!

You absolutely cannot go wrong by surrounding yourself with greenery. You just needed some information about plant care to make living in an urban jungle a possibility.

You now know that choosing the right houseplant is your first step to success. If the plant you're eyeing is in a bad state, you're starting off on the wrong foot. As a new plant parent, there's nothing like failure to crush your dreams. So, before you buy a plant, make sure it is nice and bushy, and if you spot one with a new leaf unfurling, that is even better. You're looking for leaves in abundance with no brown or yellow spots, or crispy edges.

Check for thick roots that are strong and firm. You will have to remove the plant from the pot to do this, and that is okay. Just work gently so as not to injure the plant.

I always imagine myself as Professor Pomona Sprout in *Harry Potter and the Chamber of Secrets* (Rowling, 2000) when I check for healthy roots. She pulls the mandrake from the pot to expose, healthy, yet screaming roots. Luckily, I've yet to come across any screaming roots in real life.

Brown and mushy roots are signs of overwatering and consequent root rot, and without some intervention, such plants won't survive. As a new plant parent, it is best to put such plants back on the shelf.

Roots all over the place are also not ideal. If you can see roots pushing through the top of the soil and poking out the drainage holes, then it's a sign that the plant is pot-bound. This does indicate that the plant was living in the perfect conditions to grow, but the problem is it's probably starved of nutrients.

The roots are forced to push its source of nutrition—the soil—out of the pot. Not only will they fail to get all minerals they need, but they also won't be able to absorb enough water. If there's no soil in the pot, how will they get a drink? Any water you give them will just drain right through.

As you can imagine, this puts the plant in a very stressful situation. Add to that moving it to a new home where it has to acclimatize, and it will almost certainly not make it.

Also, keep an eye out for bugs, or you'll end up bringing some unwanted visitors' home with you.

When your plant is home, lighting, watering, temperature, and humidity should be your top concerns. All these elements will vary from plant to plant, so do some research on your newly purchased houseplant.

Most plants will need a bright spot to be happy, while others will put up with lower-light conditions.

When it comes to watering, remember that less is more. Overwatering is the number one killer of houseplants. Water does not equal love, especially not if your plant is a succulent.

Temperature-wise, if you're comfortable and not too hot or cold, your plant will be okay. Unless, of course, you have one of the many heat-loving houseplants out there. Then you'll have to bump up the thermostat somewhat, but not too much. Most plants don't like dry air and prefer high moisture levels in the atmosphere. If you live in a centrally heated home, compensate for the dryness by using a humidifier. You can also place tropical-type plants in the kitchen or bathroom where the air is generally more humid.

To have happy plants, you have to mimic their natural environment. They'll thank you with new leaf after new leaf and even some beautiful flowers!

I also hope this book alleviated some of your fears about repotting plants. It is something you won't be able to avoid, especially if your plant is thriving. Fast growers outgrow their pots quickly when given the right conditions. If you want your plant to stay healthy, a bigger container is a must. Pot-bound plants find it difficult to absorb water, and as the soil gets pushed out by the roots, taking up nutrients will be near impossible.

If your plant is too big to repot (lucky you), you can replenish the soil by top dressing—just remove the first few inches off the old soil and replace it with a fresh batch. As you water, the good stuff will trickle down and give your plant the nutrient boost it needs.

In *Houseplants 101*, I also covered how you can incorporate your plants into your home decorating style. By strategically selecting plants with different leaf shapes and textures and pairing them with the right containers, you can improve a room's character. For example, angular and spiky plants pair well with more masculine designs, while plants with round and colorful leaves work well in feminine spaces.

Naturally, there may be those among you who like the contrast of hard edges with softer elements. There really are no hard and fast rules. After all, it is your home, and if you think placing a lemon tree in a pink polka dot pot looks good, go for it.

I do encourage you to go the DIY-route when it comes to matching containers with your style. Planters are expensive, particularly if they have fancy or aesthetic design components. With a can of paint, some tape, rope and a glue gun, you can make plastic pots look like big-ticket items. A good dose of imagination with a side of creativity, and you're well on your way to planter paradise.

Here's an idea: Go antique hunting and look for curious containers. As the saying goes, one person's trash is another's treasure. You can even turn an old suitcase into a retro planter. Place it on the ground in front of larger plants or give it height by attaching legs to the bottom of the suitcase.

To one person, a ramshackle chest of drawers is firewood, to an innovative plant parent, it's the perfect container for house-plants. Or, why not turn it into a planter for an indoor edible garden?

I trust that this book showed you that you don't have to limit your green thumb to ordinary houseplants. Once you have the basics of plant care down, you can literally branch out into growing your own fruits, vegetables, herbs, and edible flowers.

Not only is it gratifying to grow your food, but it is a good way to eat healthily while helping the environment. It's better to know what exactly you're putting into your body. Food labels can be misleading, and you may end up eating toxic chemicals that will harm your health in the long run. And, by setting up your own indoor edible garden, you will play your part in reducing the negative impact commercially produced foods have on the environment.

Mass-produced fruits and veggies have to travel miles to reach the store, massively contributing to carbon emissions and general air pollution. You also won't get the freshest, flavor-packed produce this way.

So, it doesn't matter if you live in a large house or a tiny apartment; growing an edible garden indoors is an option you should explore. Being a farmer is not a requirement, but resourcefulness is.

After reading this book, you know how to care for common houseplants. But I want you to remember: It doesn't matter if it is an ordinary houseplant, a fruit tree, or vegetable, plant care still stays the same. If you keep lighting, water, soil, and environmental conditions in mind, a plant is a plant is a plant.

Well, we've come to the end of this very informative book. Hopefully, you're armed with enough knowledge to feel confident in starting your indoor jungle. I hope you're excited and not fearful anymore. If you can't put the assassination of past plants out of your mind, chalk it up to inexperience.

Now that you are more knowledgeable about houseplants and their needs, success is guaranteed.

Welcome to the plant parent club and happy planting!

Thank you for reading my book. If you have enjoyed reading it perhaps you would like to leave a star rating and a review for me on Amazon? It really helps support writers like myself create more books. You can leave a review for me by scanning the QR code below:

Thank you so much.

Peter Shepperd

REFERENCES

Figure 1: Pflung, S. (n.d.). Home is where my plants are [Photograph]. *Burst.* https://burst.shopify.com/photos/home-is-where-my-plants-are?q=house+plants

Figure 2: Kumar, S. (n.d.). Indoor plant green [Photograph]. *Pixabay.* https://pixabay.com/photos/indoor-plant-green-plant-indoor-4751068/

Figure 3: Oh, C. (2019). Green dumbcane plants on brown clay pot [Photograph]. *Unsplash.* https://unsplash.com/photos/u9MM5mcML2Q

Figure 4: Tammarazzi. (n.d.). Wandering Jew houseplant [Photograph]. *Pixabay.* https://pixabay.com/photos/wandering-jew-houseplant-plant-3401913/

Figure 5: Kuptsove, A. (n.d.). Fitonnia variegated [Photograph]. *Pixabay.* https://pixabay.com/photos/fittonia-variegated-leaves-1458809/

Figure 6: Ahmadnejad, E. (n.d.). Close-up decoration environment [Photograph]. *Pixabay.* https://pixabay.com/photos/close-up-decoration-environment-3636977/

Figure 7: De Lotz, G. (2017). Hearth-shaped green leaves [Photograph]. *Unsplash.* https://unsplash.com/photos/6s7l_gTc4T0

Figure 8: Phan, H. (2019). Green leaves with holes [Photograph]. *Unsplash.* https://unsplash.com/photos/6gTtlfbBGdE

Figure 9: Photorama. (n.d.). Plant indoor natural [Photograph]. *Pixabay.* https://pixabay.com/photos/plant-indoor-natural-green-4638286/

Figure 10: Kumar, S. (n.d.). Indoor plant green [Photograph]. *Pixabay.* https://pixabay.com/photos/indoor-plant-green-plant-indoor-4751068/

Figure 11: Tranmautritam. (2016). Adult Siberian husky [Photograph]. *Pexels.* https://www.pexels.com/photo/adorable-animal-beautiful-blur-245033

Figure 12: Reddekopp, J. (2020). Brown wooden trunk with orange leaves [Photograph]. *Unsplash.* https://unsplash.com/photos/IDsTpe_DeZw

Figure 13: Lara, C. (2018). Green cherries [Photograph]. *Unsplash.* https://unsplash.com/photos/AXCUmRNTQOo

Figure 14: Noblet, E. (2017). Green plant [Photograph]. *Unsplash.* https://unsplash.com/photos/9YpzV6czaAI

Figure 15: Keefe, I. (2017). Selective focus [Photograph]. *Unsplash.* https://unsplash.com/photos/pbwPh9vfpuY

Figure 16: Kirsh, A. (n.d.). Messy indoor gardening [Photograph]. *Burst.* https://burst.shopify.com/photos/messy-indoor-gardening?q=house+plants

Figure 17: Sheldon, J. (2014). Succulent plants in glass terrarium. *Unsplash.* https://unsplash.com/photos/rDLBArZUl1c

Figure 18: Mutzi. (2019). Five plants hanging on wall [Photograph]. *Unsplash.* https://unsplash.com/photos/ZQm_wg8jxhI/info

Figure 19: Sahu, N. (2018). Green-leafed plant on white pot [Photograph]. *Pexels.* https://www.pexels.com/photo/green-leafed-plant-on-white-pot-1679014/

Figure 20: Pflug, S. (n.d.). Bringing the outside in [Photograph]. *Burst.* https://burst.shopify.com/photos/bringing-the-outside-in?q=house+plants

Gomes, F., Silva, G. & De Castro, I. (2017). Effect of home vegetable gardening on the household availability of fruits and

vegetables. *Scielo.* https://www.scielo.br/scielo.php?script=
sci_arttext&pid=S1415-52732017000200245

Lee, M., Lee, J., Park, B., & Miyazaki, Y. (2015). Interaction
with indoor plants may reduce psychological and physiological
stress by suppressing autonomic nervous system activity in
young adults: A randomized crossover study. *US National
Library of Medicine National Institute of Health.* https://
www.ncbi.nlm.nih.gov/pmc/articles/PMC4419447/

Levine, D. (n.d.). Cacti and succulents. *The University of Cali-
fornia.* http://ucce.ucdavis.edu/universal/
printedprogpageshow.cfm?pagenum=6142&progkey=
2080&county=5576

O'kane, N. (2011). Poisonous to Pets: Plants Poisonous to Dogs
and Cats. *CSIRO Publishing.*

Perry, L. (n.d.). Benefits of using plants indoors. *University of
Vermont Department of Plant and Soil Science.* http://pss.
uvm.edu/ppp/articles/healthyin.html

Pollen, M. (2013). The intelligent plant: Scientists debate a new
way of understanding flora. *The New Yorker.* https://www.
newyorker.com/magazine/2013/12/23/the-intelligent-plant

Rauh, V., Garcia, W., Whyatt, R., Horton, M., Barr, D. & Louis.
(2005). Prenatal exposure to the organophosphate pesticide
chlorpyrifos and childhood tremor. *Neuro Toxicology,* Vol. 51,

80-86. https://www.ncbi.nlm.nih.gov/pmc/articles/PMC4809635/

Rowling, J.K. (2000). Harry Potter and the Chamber of Secrets. *Scholastic Paperbacks.*

U.S. Food & Drug Administration. (2019, August 19). Lovely lilies and curious cats: A dangerous combination. https://www.fda.gov/animal-veterinary/animal-health-literacy/lovely-lilies-and-curious-cats-dangerous-combination

American Society for Prevention of Cruelty to Animals. (n.d.). Toxic and non-toxic plant list. https://www.aspca.org/pet-care/animal-poison-control/toxic-and-non-toxic-plants

Capillary action. (n.d.). Science Encyclopedia. https://science.jrank.org/pages/1182/Capillary-Action.html

Dich, J., Zahm, S., Hanberg, A. & Adami, H. (1997). Pesticides and cancer. *Pubmed.* https://pubmed.ncbi.nlm.nih.gov/9498903/

Epiphyte. (1998). Encyclopaedia Britannica. https://www.britannica.com/plant/epiphyte